the Gentle Breeze of Jesus

Mel and Nona Tari

D1603612

NEW LEAF PRESS
Box 1045 Harrison, Ark 72601

We wish to thank
George Otis and Cliff Dudley
for encouraging us to write this book in the first place,
and
Beth Tebbe and Delores Bauer
for their valuable suggestions.

We especially want to thank Cliff Dudley for spending hours helping us transform the rough draft into a finished manuscript and for being a source of much needed encouragement and advice.

Biblical quotations, unless otherwise noted,
are reprinted with permission from the New American Standard Bible
© 1971 by the Lockman Foundation.

Printed in the United States of America

First printing—July 1974 (10,000)
Second printing—November 1974 (5,000)
First printing—September 1975 (20,000)
Second printing—July 1976 (20,000)
Third printing—June 1977 (20,000)

NEW LEAF EDITION
First printing—September 1978 (10,000)
Second printing—September 1979 (10,000)
Third printing—May 1980 (7,500)
Fourth printing—July 1981 (5,000)
Fifth printing—February 1982 (5,000)
Sixth printing—March 1983 (5,000)
Seventh printing—April 1984 (5,000)

ISBN 0-89221-056-7
Library of Congress Catalog Card Number 78-64960

Lovingly dedicated
to
the Hero of the Indonesian revival,
who is
our God, Friend, and Lover,

JESUS.

Contents

Publisher's Foreword

Mel Tari, now known on six continents as an eyewitness chronicler of the Indonesian revival, was born on March 18, 1946, in the village of Niki-niki on the island of Timor. He was the third of ten children of an elementary-school principal and his wife, both Christians.

His childhood was spent in another village, Pene, and in Soe, a mountain town of about five thousand. At the age of fifteen, he entered high school in the island's capital and port city, Kupang. He was graduated in late 1964 from Christian High School in Waikabubak on the nearby island of Sumba, a Reformed Church academy.

His scholastic record drew the attention of the Sukarno government, which at that time was busily arranging college opportunities in the Soviet Union. Mel was offered a full seven-year scholarship for either electronic or medical studies at a Moscow university. He accepted, then returned to his parents in Timor for a short interval before leaving.

The first flickers of revival were bringing changes to the Maryland-sized island, however. Mel, despite his Christian heritage and education, was not yet a believer. An evangelistic crusade in Soe produced healings which he could not explain, and sometime later he made his personal decision for Christ.

By August, 1965, when he should have left for Moscow, he had declined the scholarship.

The renewal exploded with full force in the Soe church the night of September 26, 1965, when the New Testament phenomena of the Day of Pentecost were repeated—a tornadolike wind, visible fire (which prompted police in their station across the street to set off the fire alarm and summon volunteer firefighters), and numerous conversions as well as infillings with the Holy Spirit, complete with speaking in tongues, including English. By midnight, teams of laymen had been organized to begin spreading the gospel the next day.

Four days later, on September 30, 1965, army insurgents in Jakarta launched the coup which was to have turned Indonesia into a communist state. It failed, and after much bloodshed, Sukarno was deposed.

Such uncertainty forced the Timorese Christians to rely ever more strongly on their new-found spiritual courage. Mel was eventually assigned to Team 42 and spent the next five years in full-time ministry throughout his island and others nearby.

Convinced that God wanted him to share a message with American Christians, Mel landed in Los Angeles September 1, 1970. He spent the next nine months in itinerant speaking, astounding audiences with his accounts of miracles in response to simple faith. He then left for Europe for six weeks before returning home.

His book, *Like a Mighty Wind*, written with Cliff Dudley, was published in late 1971 and dominated the best-seller charts for the next year. To date, 250,000 hardback copies are in print, and a 100,000-copy paperback edition has just been released. Spanish, Dutch, Swedish, Danish, German, Icelandic, British, Afrikaans, Norwegian, Portuguese, and Finnish editions have pushed total sales over half a million.

Reviewers' reactions were strong and divided. "Miracles are happening today in Indonesia," noted the *Baptist Record*, while the *Conservative Baptist* called the book "an unfortunate and gross distortion . . . a perfect example of an imaginative mentality unchecked by facts and the Word." According to the *Bulletin of the Scottish Institute of Missionary Studies*, "The obvious sincerity of the author cannot be doubted," while American missionary statesman W. Stanley Mooneyham insisted the book had quoted him out of context and wrote: "People . . . want to know if I do indeed endorse the book. The simple answer is: I do not." His article in *World Vision* was widely reprinted.

Meanwhile, Mel Tari returned to the United States via Asia, Africa, and Europe. On May 29, 1972, he was married to Nona Rea, daughter of former Moody Bible Institute professor Dr. John Rea. The young couple returned in September, 1972, to set up their home in Soe and participate in the ongoing revival, then some seven years running.

A year later, they came to this country for further speaking engagements and also to write the present volume, *The Gentle Breeze of Jesus*.

As with *Like a Mighty Wind*, this second book must be seen as the spontaneous, unpretentious expression of an Indonesian Christian. He has neither the temperament nor the motivation to deceive us. Mel Tari is understandably foreign to the skepticism and pessimism of Western thought. He is more interested in letting us know that the wind of the Spirit has not calmed in Timor, that the churches continue in a state of renewal and evangelism, than in placing any given miracle under scrutiny and exhausting the hypotheses for natural explanations.

His teachings will again appear to many readers to be effusive, even childish. He simply speaks from his own experience at making the Scriptures relevant to his daily life and ministry. He is a challenge to more sophisticated minds to reconsider the words of our Lord: "Whoever does not receive the kingdom of God like a child shall not enter it at all" (Mark 10:15).

Preface

As Mel Tari's wife, I have had the privilege of living in Soe, the town where the Indonesian revival started nine years ago. I've been able to observe the team members who for years have been faithfully preaching the gospel all over the island of Timor and the big country of Indonesia. It was a thrill to become personally acquainted with many of the people mentioned in the book *Like a Mighty Wind*. These very people are the ones God has used, and is still using, to do tremendous miracles.

I have had the unique opportunity of seeing the more intimate sides of the revival from an American point of view. After living and talking with the people who have played some of its major roles, I discovered that I had many misconceptions about what the revival is really like. (I believe many people throughout the Western world have these same mistaken ideas.)

My first big surprise was to find out that the Indonesian revival is *not* an American revival. I imagined, before I arrived there for the first time, that Soe would be in a state of constant excitement. People would call to their friends, "Hey, did you hear about the latest miracle?" Of course, everybody in the village would know exactly what was going on. News about the revival would be the main topic of conversation. When a

Communion service was announced (for which the Lord had changed water to wine), people from all over the island would crowd into the big church in Soe to get a firsthand glimpse of what the Lord had done.

But this is the American way of doing things. It would be impossible for extraordinary miracles like the multiplying of food, raising of the dead, and changing of water to wine to happen in America without creating a lot of excitement. Within half an hour several newspapermen would be on the scene, and possibly even a few TV cameras. Americans as a people have a vivacious, inquisitive personality. They are outgoing and love to discuss the unusual.

Indonesians are just the opposite. They are reserved. They much prefer quietness and peace to a lot of excitement, and it takes something phenomenal to arouse them from their placidity. Yet they have the tremendous quality of stability. They might not get as outwardly excited about their Christian life as some Americans do, but they possess a faithfulness and perseverance that brings them out far ahead in the long run.

So when I entered Soe for the first time, the town looked unbelievably quiet. The humdrum of daily life seemed to have swept away all traces of the revival. There was no sign of any miracles. In fact, it would be possible for someone to stay for a while in Soe without knowing that a tremendous moving of God was taking place all around him.

However, for someone who is spiritually perceptive, there are many evidences to give the secret away. One of the first things I noticed was the unusual church attendance. Sunday after Sunday, rain or shine, the big church building that seats fifteen hundred was totally packed out. Then the first congregation was dismissed and an entirely new group of people took their place. Every Sunday three thousand people squeezed into the big church. That's a remarkable proportion for a town of five thousand with three other thriving churches in the immediate area. The worshipers themselves impressed me with their fervency. I don't remember ever before seeing a group of believers so united in spirit and so hungry for God's Word.

My second discovery is closely related to the first. Indonesian Christians do *not* talk about miracles—except to the person they consider their spiritual advisor. An example of this occurred in January of 1973. Shortly after New Year's Day the Lord once again changed water to wine for a Communion service. Eight hundred people participated. But nobody talked about the miracle the Lord had just performed. Mel and I were living just a block or two away from the church, but we didn't find out what was going on until it was too late to attend. (The Communion service had been announced the Sunday before in the second service, while we had attended the first.) Mel believes that even some of the people drinking the Communion wine didn't know exactly where it came from. The pastor didn't publicize the fact that it had been miraculously converted from water.

When a stranger questions the team members, they are very hesitant to talk about the wonderful things they've seen God do. For one thing, they are shy and find it difficult to talk about personal matters with someone they do not yet know and trust. The Indonesian Christians also have a fear of robbing God of some of this glory by setting the persons He has used on a pedestal. For that reason they confide only in their spiritual leader or their closest friend. Since so many of the team members consider my husband to be their spiritual father, Mel has been able to collect hundreds of stories about the revival. He knows more than anyone else about the great things the Lord has been doing on the island of Timor these past nine years.

I believe God has been able to do so many astounding things in Timor because the people *do not* talk about His miracles. There is always a danger that Christians will take their eyes off the Lord and instead fasten them on what He does. This is enough to grind any revival to a halt. The Timorese Christians have sidestepped this danger by keeping the Lord Jesus and

His love uppermost in their minds and by assigning miracles to their proper place in the background.

My third surprise was to find that not all the sick people in Timor, or even in Soe for that matter, have been healed. I remember the day I heard about a little baby who had been born deformed in a nearby village. Its left arm was only a stub, a tiny finger sticking out of the arm socket. My friend, whom I call Tanta Ete, went to visit the baby's family. While she was gone, all I could think about was the Lord doing a great miracle to heal the baby. Tanta Ete told me after returning home how she had prayed with the baby's grandfather, helping him to renounce the demonic activities in which he had been involved. The Lord had revealed to my friend that the grandfather was the cause of the baby's deformity.

"But Tanta Ete," I quickly blurted out, "didn't you pray for the baby's healing?"

She gave me a blank look, almost as if that thought had never entered her head. Evidently it wasn't God's time to heal the baby. My friend didn't make the mistake of "claiming by faith" that the Lord would do something which He did not yet want to do. This is one of the powerful principles of the Indonesian revival—the principle of simple faith: finding out exactly what God wants to do in each situation and then setting Him free to do it by simple obedience. Since we feel this principle is so vital to a true move of God, we have devoted chapter three entirely to its discussion.

Many people whom we've met in our travels around the world have the mistaken idea that the Timorese church is a perfect church, somehow better than their own. I am very proud of the Indonesian Christians. I feel they have learned many valuable spiritual lessons which could benefit the churches in other parts of the world. The Christians in America, for instance, have much to learn from the Christians in Timor. But the reverse is also true. In their unique relationship with God, Americans have discovered spiritual insights which the Timorese need to learn. In other words, none of us are perfectly mature or self-sufficient; we all have much to learn from one another. We should never make the mistake of putting a certain group of people on a pedestal in God's eyes. We all are equal.

In this book Mel and I would like to describe to you some of the experiences of our friends in Indonesia. We are sharing the truths that the Lord has revealed to them, which have become a part of their everyday life. We hope you will absorb these truths just as readily as the Indonesian Christians would absorb the things you have to share with them.

This book does not exhaust the supply of stories to be told about the Indonesian revival. The longer I live in Timor, the more amazed I become at all that the Lord has done and is still doing today. I am thrilled that the Lord can work so quietly and yet accomplish so much, leaving such deep, lasting results. As Mel and I attempt to record the things the Lord has done, we share somewhat in the frustrations of John, the Gospel writer. To paraphrase his closing remark: "There are also many other things which Jesus did—and is doing—in Indonesia, which if they were written in detail, I suppose that even the world itself would not contain the books which were written."

NONA TARI

1
The Greatest Miracle

Timor . . . it was in these rugged, rocky hills that one day I bumped smack into the Lord Jesus Christ. And I tell you, my life could never be the same again.

You see, one day in 1965, the Lord started a mighty revival in my island. The Holy Spirit came down on us with His power and love just like He did in the book of Acts. And, oh, He did such wonderful things for us.

We were a cold, dead bunch of people before that, but Jesus loved us anyway. And I tell you, when we got to know Jesus—I mean, to really know Him face to face—it changed us.

We started to get terribly excited about our wonderful Master. If you were bored stiff sitting in church every Sunday, and all of a sudden you became a close friend of the Lord Jesus and found out that He was doing today the very same things He did in the Bible, you'd get excited too!

Maybe you have heard about the miracles the Lord Jesus did for us. Yes, it's true, I have seen Him do some tremendously wonderful things: heal sick people . . . save thousands of souls . . . change water into wine for our Communion services . . . multiply our food . . . raise several people from the dead—oh, there's just so much to tell you about.

I remember one night especially. Soon after the revival

started I was in Noenoni with my team. We were having special meetings in the little church in the middle of the village.

(In Timor, our churches look exactly like all the other houses, except they're a little bigger. But you don't even know what the houses look like yet, so I guess I'd better tell you. I think they're real cute. They always look so sleepy to me. The walls are made of gray palm branches. They lean and sag as if they just can't manage to stand up straight. The gray shutters on the little windows swing open and shut in the wind—it seems like the little house is blinking at you. The door is often left wide-open in a big yawn. And then finally there's a big huge grass roof that's trying hard to balance on top of everything else. Actually it's way too top-heavy. You get the feeling that any minute the whole house might crumple to the ground, where it can sleep in peace forever. But, thank the Lord, it never quite does.)

That night the little church was packed out. All the wobbly wooden benches were full of ladies, so the men just sat on the dirt floor. When the floor was full, the rest of the people who came late had to stand around outside and try to peek in through the windows.

Well, after we were done preaching, we asked if anybody wanted prayer for healing. Right away a mother came up to us with her seventeen-year-old son.

Now what's wrong with him? I thought. *He looks like any normal, healthy boy to me.*

But the mother had tears in her eyes. She told us that ever since her son was born he had been both blind and deaf, and so of course he couldn't talk either.

Then the poor mother started to cry real hard. "Oh, I'm so desperate," she sobbed. "Oh, I want Jesus to heal my boy."

All the other Christians in the little church looked like they were ready to cry too. I guess everyone in the village really loved that boy; they all wished he could have a normal, happy life. Later the pastor told me that all evening he had been praying in his heart, "O Lord, heal Gabriel! Even if you don't

14

do anything else tonight, O Lord, please heal Gabriel."

After we had been praying just a few minutes the Lord spoke to my team leader's heart. He gave her the gift of knowledge. "This boy's great-great-grandfather was very wicked," my team leader told everyone. "He was a real hero in the tribal wars, but he got all his power from the demons. One day he decided to offer a victory sacrifice to the devil. So he took a little baby and buried it alive in a swamp. Did you ever hear about this? Does this story make any sense to you?" she asked.

"Oh, yes," the mother and all the other friends answered. "We know all about it. Everything you said is very true."

"Well," my team leader went on, "the Lord has shown me that this is why Gabriel is blind and deaf. A demonic curse has been passed on to him from his great-great-grandfather! But praise the Lord, our God has all power over the devil."

So right away we all agreed in faith and renounced the demonic curse in the name of Jesus. Then we asked the Lord to not only set him free, but to do a total job—to heal him from the top of his fuzzy head to the tips of his little brown toes.

And can you guess what happened? The Lord Jesus really answered our prayers that night. Gabriel was healed instantly! His eyes opened real big and he looked all around him. He stared at the dirt floor with such an amazed look on his face that it seemed like he thought it was made out of gold. He stroked the little wooden bench he was sitting on as if it were a fancy throne. I guess he felt like he had been transported to heaven!

And when we started to talk to him, his face just shone with joy. The more we talked, the bigger he smiled. But what thrilled us the most was the way he started to talk right away, even though he had never heard a single word in his life. I guess the Holy Spirit Himself was his private schoolteacher. He started out with real simple words like *mamma* and *papa*. But pretty soon he was talking whole sentences.

His quiet, dark world had suddenly become very noisy and terribly, terribly interesting. Everything fascinated him—an ant crawling around on the floor, the big kerosene pressure lamp hanging from the rafters (he thought it was the sun!), his mother's soft happy voice.

Everybody there in the church was so happy and excited. We couldn't stop thanking the Lord. I kept thinking about what Jesus had said two thousand years ago. But that night with my own eyes I had seen Him prove that it still works today: "And everything you ask in prayer, believing, you shall receive" (Matthew 21:22).

In August of 1970 two of my friends from Chicago came to visit me here in Soe. They didn't know it ahead of time, but Jesus had a nice surprise up His sleeve; He had planned a real big blessing for them. You see, we had been planning to have a Communion service, and they came just in time to get in on it.

We didn't have any wine to serve, but we weren't one bit worried. We knew Jesus would supply our needs. He had already told us He was going to change water to wine for us. And He had given us all the instructions of what we were supposed to do.

So one day a group of ladies went down to a spring of water in Kampung Aman—that's a little village right next to Soe. They filled a big pot with water, covered it, and then brought it back to their house. The Lord had told us to gather in their house to pray every night for three nights in a row. On the third night He'd change it to wine.

But do you know what? During this whole time my two American friends were very busy. They had given themselves the job of being "checker"—they wanted to make sure no funny business went on. One of them took a separate glass of water from the spring and carried it back to his own room. Every day he inspected it. He kept saying to himself, *Now maybe there are some minerals in here. Maybe there's a good scientific explanation. Maybe it won't be a real miracle after all.* (He was a funny brother; he made me laugh and laugh. He sort of

16

reminded me of doubting Thomas.)

After three days the water in his glass was still plain old ordinary water—except it didn't taste as fresh as our good spring water usually does. But that night when my two friends and I went to the house to pray, we found out that a wonderful miracle really *had* happened and there wasn't any scientific explanation either. The Lord had gone beyond the laws of nature and had changed that water to a nice reddish-colored wine.

(Sometimes people ask me, "Now is it really wine or is it grape juice?" I have to answer them this way: "It's both and it's neither. It's a heavenly recipe. It has a strong smell like wine. But like grape juice, there's no alcohol in it. So if you want to, you can either call it 'nonalcoholic wine' or 'extra-smelly grape juice.' ")

When my two friends saw what the Lord had done, they didn't have any choice. They had to believe that the power of God is real.

I remember one evening in December of 1965. All that day the seven other guys on my team and I had been walking and walking. We walked so far it seemed like my legs were going to fall off. We climbed steep, rocky trails that had the sharpest stones my brown bare feet ever stepped on. We trudged through big fields of scrubby grass on the sides of the mountains. They seemed like they were made out of elastic—the farther we walked the bigger they stretched.

And wow! that sun was really hot! Before we started out I looked up at the sky and said, "Hi, sun. My, you look nice and warm and friendly today." But before we had walked an hour I found that the sun was *too* friendly. I was so thirsty that I wished I could swallow a lake. And my head felt like a hard-boiled egg or something.

Well, anyway, finally off in the distance, sitting on the side of a hill, we saw the village Jesus had told us to walk to. Its name

17

was Baob. Was I ever glad to see it! You'd better believe me, by then I was ready to quit.

But then a wonderful thing happened. I remember that by the time we entered the little village, the sun was setting. He was sliding down behind the purple hills to go to bed. The whole sky was dancing for joy, waving banners of red and pink and gold. That evening the sun painted such a beautiful picture for us that I couldn't help forgive him for all the misery he'd given me.

The first thing we did was to head straight for the pastor's house. But before any of us had taken one single step over the stone wall that was running around his house and garden, the Lord spoke to my team leader. "No! Don't you go in there to sleep tonight! I want all eight of you to sleep right over there under that big tree."

When my team leader told us the news, I was stunned. "What! Sleep on the hard, cold ground tonight? I already ache so bad it feels like my bones have lost their hinges. How in the world can I ever preach tomorrow?" I tell you, I really felt awful.

But after I had grumbled around for a while, Jesus started speaking real softly in my heart. "Mel, I left my beautiful palace in heaven to come to earth just for you. I slept on the hard ground lots of times. Is this such a big sacrifice to make for Me?"

"Oh, Lord Jesus!" I felt terribly ashamed of myself. "I'm so sorry! I can never possibly make too big a sacrifice for You. Thank You for this little chance to prove I love You."

So that night, under the twinkling stars, I lay my head down on a stone pillow and decided to pretend I was Jacob. And as I closed my eyes to go to sleep, I felt Jesus smiling at me.

Very early the next morning, just as soon as the first roosters started screeching hello, we all woke up. It was so cold we just couldn't sleep anymore. (You can't imagine how cold it can get in the Timorese mountains at night!) Some of the other guys found some dry sticks and leaves. Pretty soon we were all sitting around a nice hot fire trying to warm up.

Before long a strange-looking man came walking up to us. He had long, greasy hair—it looked like he had never cut it in his whole life. He had wound it round and round on his head in a big bun to keep it out of the way. And one of his eyes looked funny. It had white film over it, and it just stared straight ahead without moving around like it was supposed to. It was probably blind.

He told us a very strange story. "We still haven't had any rain here, even though the rainy season should have started two months ago. All the people are afraid they'll starve. So I've been praying to the devil and offering sacrifices so he'll give us rain. He and I are real good friends and usually he answers me right away. But this time he won't.

"One day, after I had offered a chicken to the devil, I had a very unusual dream. I heard a voice say to me, 'For a long time the devil has been stealing My rain. But I won't let him do it anymore. He can't give you any rain from now on, no matter how hard you pray.'

"And it's true. No matter what I do, the devil won't give me any rain. I keep offering him bigger and bigger sacrifices —chickens, roosters, goats—and every single time I have the same dream.

"Yesterday I finally took a cow to my most sacred altar on top of Mount Mutis." (That's the highest mountain in Timor.) "When I came home to go to sleep, I had that same dream again. But this time the voice added, 'I've told you before you wouldn't get any rain, but you didn't believe Me. Everything you try to do is useless. But if you go to the big tree in the village of Baob early tomorrow morning, you will find eight of My servants. They will tell you what to do.'

"So that's why I'm here right now. Please tell me, who is the real God? The voice who talked to me? I'm at my wits' end. What does He want me to do?"

We explained to him that it was the Lord Jesus Christ who was talking to him. He wanted him to repent and become a

Christian. Then we told him the beautiful story of salvation—how the heavenly Father loved us so much, even though we were sinners, that He sent His Son Jesus to earth to die for us and take away our sins.

We had hardly finished the story when the pagan priest fell on his knees and started to pray. "O Lord Jesus, I want You. I've been so awfully wicked. But please forgive me. Please make my black heart white and clean. Jesus, I want You to be my Master forever and ever."

I tell you, it's an awesome and thrilling thing to watch a new baby being born into God's family. I could just imagine how the angels were singing and praising around the throne of God.

When the man had finished talking with the Lord, his face was sparkling with that beautiful joy that only Jesus can give. But then he asked us, "Can Jesus heal my blind eye? The demons heal other people when I ask them to, but they can't heal me. If I ask Jesus to heal me, will He do it?"

Of course we said yes, and we prayed for him right away. Oh, praise our wonderful Jesus, he was healed instantly. He told us he could see perfectly out of that eye for the first time in many years. And it even looked different! It didn't look dead and funny anymore. But in just a second Jesus had recreated it to look just like the other one.

Then the man said, "I have one more request. Can you pray that the Lord will give us rain?"

"We will pray," we answered, "but it won't rain here until we finish preaching in this village. Otherwise nobody will come to the meetings." It was really wonderful! The very day we left, the rain poured down out of heaven so hard that everybody knew it had to be a miracle.

But the biggest miracle of all was how that dear man's life was changed. I tell you, it really makes me proud of my Jesus to see how He can transform someone so terribly awful into one of His most precious children.

That very day the man asked us to cut off his long hair. And

20

boy, you'd better believe me, that's a sure proof that he really repented. In Timor the pagan priests never cut their hair. They're very proud of it—it's sort of like their trademark. It's a sign that they've gone all-out for the devil. (I took some of his long hair to keep as a souvenir. But I think I've lost it by now.)

Then the man went over to the pastor's house to make friends with him. For years he had hated the pastor and had tried to do everything he could think of to bug the poor guy and wreck his ministry. When the pastor found out that his worst enemy had accepted the Lord, he was so happy he could have cried.

(Do you know what I found out? If we had slept in the pastor's house like we'd wanted to, that man would never have gotten saved. He hated the pastor so much that he couldn't stand even to put a big toe in his front door, no matter how badly he wanted to find out who that voice was that was talking to him. So you see, Jesus didn't make us suffer for nothing. My Master is so smart. We can trust Him that He always knows best when He tells us to do something.)

And then can you guess what the former pagan priest did? He asked us to change his name; he couldn't stand his old pagan name any longer. It used to be Oe, which means "water" in Timorese. (It's an animistic custom to be named after trees, mountains, snakes, and so on.) But he asked us to call him Willem instead. That was the pastor's name, and he wanted to be like the pastor—a real man of God instead of a servant of the devil.

Willem brought a huge pile of fetishes and demonic stuff to the pastor's house to be burned. And then he started witnessing all around the countryside. Before he was saved he had been one of the most powerful heathen priests in Timor. So you can imagine what an impact his testimony had on everyone. In his own village at least two hundred people got saved after seeing the change in him.

How we praised the Lord! This was really a great breakthrough. Before, the people had been so scared of him that even if they had wanted to become Christians they wouldn't do it. He'd tell the demons to send rats to eat up all their corn so they'd starve. But from then on until he died in 1972, Willem was a real leader for Jesus.

Oh, how wonderful our precious Lord Jesus is. We should never ever limit His power in any way. *Nothing*, and I mean absolutely nothing, is impossible for Him to do.

Yes, miracles are exciting. No matter how many times I've seen the Lord's power at work, it never gets boring. I can never get tired of watching Him do something wonderful.

But I want to tell you something with all my heart. Miracles are exciting, *but they're not half as exciting as the Lord Jesus Himself.*

I had better admit something to you: I'm terribly in love with my Jesus! Sometimes when I sit down and think about how delightful and irresistible He is, I can hardly breathe. It just takes my breath away to think that this infinitely precious Jesus belongs to me. Oh, I tell you my greatest desire and goal in this life is to get to know Him better—to discover all the facets of His wonderful personality and to just plain get lost in the wonder of His love. If the only thing I ever had to do from now till the end of eternity was to get to know Him better, wow! That would be enough to make me completely happy!

But do you know something sad? Even though the Lord Jesus is so wonderful, some people are kind of bored with Him. They don't get half as excited about Him and His love for them as they do when they hear a real good story about a miracle. I'm afraid those people would rather have miracles than the Lord Jesus Christ. They would rather go to a meeting and see a big, super-duper miracle happen than spend an hour alone with Jesus, just talking with Him and drinking in His love.

Now I know miracles are dramatic and thrilling. As human beings we get terribly curious whenever something unusual happens. But I think there's a danger if we start to think about them too much. Pretty soon we might get all mixed up and miss the whole point of being a Christian.

My friend, the Christian life is *not* a circus. God doesn't use His power just to entertain us and give us a thrill. Jesus is not some kind of a magician. I mean, He doesn't do a miracle just to show off and to make us say, "Now I wonder how in the world He ever did that; there has to be a good explanation."

No! I believe God does miracles for only three basic reasons: to show us His great love and concern for us, to draw us closer to Himself, and to teach us more about Himself (or to "glorify Himself," to use Bible language.)

You know, I believe that many times today the Lord longs to show us His power, but He doesn't dare. He knows we might get so excited about the *things He does* that we'll forget all about *Him*.

The Lord Jesus longs for each of us to come into a real deep love relationship with Himself. He longs for us to love to spend time with Him—to love Him just for Himself because He's so desirable. Oh, it just blesses His dear heart so much when we grab every chance possible to be close to Him.

Now let me tell you a little secret. If we have this attitude toward Jesus—if He's our most precious treasure—then miracles should be a natural result of our relationship with Him. We'll get all those nice miracles, too. He is so full of power and He loves us so much that He just can't help doing wonderful things for us—if we simply submit to His Word, that is.

We had been working hard on the island of Semau for several months. But it was a real battle, because, you see, Semau is famous for being the stronghold of the witch doctors. The demonic power there is just indescribable. If the witch doctors don't like someone, they will pray to the demons and ask them to make their enemy very sick. Or sometimes if they're mad enough, the pagan priests, as we call them, will ask the demons to send lightning out of heaven and strike the enemy dead. The worst part about it is that the demonic power really works; the pagan priests get what they ask for.

But praise God, the Lord has all power over Satan, and He was really blessing our ministry. At least two hundred people had gotten saved. And at least ten of those wicked witch doctors had really repented and come to Jesus. We had some big, blazing bonfires when they burned all their *djimats* ("fetishes") and the other demonic stuff they use in their worship.

The Lord Jesus was also busy healing people. I remember there was a little kid who was born blind, and some men with huge, swollen stomachs—they looked like they were either pregnant or else had swallowed big balloons. And besides these there was a bunch of other sick people the Lord Jesus healed too.

But to be honest, I have to admit that we were really dead tired. The two other guys on my team were sort of sick because we had been working so hard day and night.

But can you imagine what my precious Jesus did? He's such a wonderful Master. He doesn't ever treat us like an old workhorse, but I believe He wants us to have fun serving Him. Well, one night after the meeting was finally over, after we had prayed for the last sick person to be healed, and after the last little old lady had finally gone home to go to bed, Jesus told us to go outside the church and sit down on the grass.

That night the moon was glowing high in the sky. It seemed to me that she was a royal queen on her throne, and the shimmering clouds all around were her long, flowing robes. She was splashing silver down on all the coconut palm trees that were gazing up at her. While I watched, she drenched the dainty bamboos with her crystal light until they were glowing like a string of pearls. The whole world had become a tropical fairyland; I couldn't help being captured by its beauty.

"My faithful sons," the Lord said to us, "I'm going to give you a little treat. I want to reward you for being such good helpers. Now look at the moon. I'm going to show you a special little 'film,' and the moon will be the screen." (Jesus was going to give each of us a vision. But the wonderful thing was that He gave all three of us the same vision at the same time.)

At first we didn't see anything. But as soon as we prayed, the Lord must have given us heavenly eyes or something, and *wow!* I'll tell you, I had never before seen such a sight.

There on the "screen" Jesus had painted some pretty green hills with a little blue stream bubbling between them. And there were lots of nice tall trees standing around raising their big leafy arms up to heaven. Then we noticed that Jesus was sitting on a big rock dressed in shepherd's clothes. All around his feet were a whole lot of cute little lambs. They were eating and sleeping, and some were hopping around playing with each other. All of a sudden Jesus stood up and started walking. All the lambs followed Him. Pretty soon they all disappeared over the other side of the hill.

Then the Lord showed us "scene two." Oh, it was just too precious for words. We saw a little lost lamb all alone, lying on the grass crying. Then the Shepherd came and picked it up in His big strong arms and held it against His heart. The little guy looked nervous at first, but the Shepherd patted him and whispered in his ears and smoothed his curly wool. Pretty soon the lamb wiggled around a little bit, and then he cuddled down in the Shepherd's arms and went to sleep.

Oh, if only you could have seen Jesus' face as He looked down at His little lamb. It was so tender and full of compassion and He was smiling the sweetest smile. He looked so happy—as if He had found His most valuable treasure.

The longer I looked at Jesus the more beautiful He became to me. But it was His eyes that really captured me. They were just so full of love—it seemed like I could almost see love pouring out of them like a fountain. When I really gazed deep into them, I almost felt like I was looking through the windows of His heart. What I saw there was so wonderful, so amazing, that it took my breath away.

His heart was like an infinitely big garden full of sweetness and a laughing, sunshiny kind of joy. There were lots of pretty flowers and trees all over Jesus' heart-garden. They were being bathed in a fountain of pure, golden love. They were just sparkling with joy, as if they were thrilled to be alive, thrilled to belong to Jesus. I know that what I saw there in Jesus' heart was so wonderful that I longed to live there forever and ever.

When the vision was over, I sat there on the grass, lost in Jesus' presence. My heart was so awed I could hardly move. To think my Jesus loved me that much! Far more even than He loved that little lamb. To think He saved me from my sin just so He could bring me home to His great loving heart to live with Him forever!

I tell you, the thrill of Jesus' love was indescribably precious to me—much more precious than all those other miracles I had seen Him do. In fact I had almost forgotten about them because my Lord Himself was so much more wonderful. I know you would have felt the same way.

2
Love-Gifts from Jesus

Now I want to ask you a question. Do you realize how terribly much the heavenly Father loves you? I mean *you*, personally? Do you know that His wonderful, loving heart is so concerned about all the problems *you* have? It doesn't matter to Him whether they are real huge or real tiny. They are all important to Him. In fact, He cares about your problems even more than you do.

He's known about them all along. But He's been waiting and waiting for you to throw the whole mess on Him so that He'll be able to fix it up real nice for you.

I tell you, the Lord has really gone out of His way to prove this to us—that He really loves us and wants to help us with *everything* in our life. In 1973, for example, we had a horrible population explosion of rats in Timor. Oh, you'd better believe me, it was just awful! Rats were all over the place. They would eat up everything until the poor farmers in the villages would starve.

One day a man was out pulling weeds in the little cornfield in front of his little palm hut. In Timor during the rainy season we plant our corn in our front yard. The corn grows so tall and fast that often all you can see of the house is the grass roof, sitting like a hat on top of a patch of waving, bobbing corn.

Well, the farmer was out in his cornfield minding his own business when all of a sudden a rat poked his head out of a hole. Real quick the farmer took his stick and banged him on the head till he died.

But pretty soon two more rats came along. The farmer banged one on the head, but the other one was too quick and ran away. I guess he went home and told all his other friends that their rat friend had been murdered. Before the farmer knew what was happening, hundreds, and I mean hundreds, of rats came pouring into his front yard. And they were really mad. They ate up everything in sight. Pretty soon his cornfield was a chewed-up mess.

The poor farmer was frantic. The more he banged them on the head, the more rats came. How would you like to have your front yard covered with rats? Ugly, thieving, mean rats?

But they didn't stop there. After they ate up everything in his garden they all ran into his house. The farmer screamed to his wife to help him light fires to smoke the rats out. That's an old trick the villagers hand down to their sons and grandsons. Usually it works real good.

But this time it didn't. The rats scurried up the walls and onto the rafters. They sat up there on their haunches and just blinked down at them like a bunch of naughty schoolboys, as if they thought the smoke smelled good!

Finally, after they were hoarse from screaming, the farmer and his wife got so desperate that they fell on their knees. (They should have done that in the first place.) "Oh, Jesus, help us! Oh, You've got to help us! Do something quick," they begged.

And can you imagine what they saw when they opened their eyes? It was such a strange sight that the farmer started to tremble. There the rats went, one by one, running down the walls and out the front door, nose touching tail, nose touching tail. And single file they hopped the stone fence around the farmer's yard. The rats never came back again.

Now that's very typical of my Jesus. He is just longing to help us if we'll only invite Him to step into our problems. As soon as we do, He'll get all His amazing power and creative wisdom going full speed in our behalf. He'll get the big wheels of the heavenly factory rolling. And pretty soon He will produce a solution that's so perfect, so fantastic, that we'd never have imagined such a wonderful thing could possibly happen to us.

But yet we're so stupid sometimes. Instead of just handing our troubles to Jesus, we worry ourselves sick. We act as if we thought God would have a nervous breakdown if He were ever put on the spot to help us out with something.

My friends, did you know that it actually insults the Lord when we worry? It's like saying to Him, "I'm sorry, Lord Jesus, but You're just not strong enough to take care of this for me. I'm afraid You're just a little bit too dumb to figure out how to get me out of this mess. I'd better try to manage it all by myself."

Oh, I tell you, we must really hurt His feelings sometimes. But our Jesus is so patient and sweet. He doesn't get mad at us. He just waits and waits until we finally get it through our thick heads that He can take care of us much better than we can ourselves.

You know, the Lord really has some cute ways of teaching us how stupid it is to worry. One day I was riding in the back of a big truck. I was going from Kupang, our capital coastal city, back home to Soe. A whole bunch of us guys had piled in on top of a big stack of junk—rice bags, big sacks of grain, some cans of kerosene, and I know there were a bunch of pigs and chickens down there somewhere too. They were tied together by their feet and, boy, it seemed to me you could have heard them and smelled them a mile away. (A couple of years ago big trucks were the only way to get anywhere in Timor—besides walking, of course. They were the fanciest limousines we had.)

Well, we were all piled together up there having a lot of fun, laughing and punching each other and telling jokes. I tell you, there's nothing we like better in Indonesia than a good hard laugh whenever something funny happens.

When we came to the pretty little town of Camplong, a

simple Timorese farmer climbed in. My! He was really a sight. He was carrying a big thirty-pound sack of grain on his shoulder. On the other shoulder he was trying to balance his big, hollow, bamboo log filled with water. (Most of the villagers don't have buckets or pails, so that's how they carry their drinking water. They put a cover over the end so the water doesn't fall out.) On top of all that he was holding six ears of dried corn tied together with a rope—he was planning to boil them with some papaya leaves to eat for lunch.

We had lurched and swayed and rattled along the rocky road for a few miles when all at once I noticed that someone behind me was panting. I craned my neck around to have a look. And do you know what? There was that poor farmer with sweat just pouring off his face, *still holding all his heavy junk*!

"My dear man! What in the world are you doing!" This was just too much for me. "Put your junk down right now."

The old guy looked down at his dusty bare feet and wiggled his big toe. Then he blushed horribly. If his brown face could have gotten red, I think it would have been as red as a hot chili pepper. Finally he whispered as softly as he could (I guess he wished no one else would hear), "Well, you see, I don't have too much money. I barely have enough to pay for myself. I don't have one single rupiah left over to pay the truck to haul my stuff. So whether I like it or not, I have to hold it."

"What!" I couldn't believe my ears! I was so shocked I almost fell off the truck. "Don't you have a bit of sense, man? If the truck's carrying you, it's carrying all your junk too. Put it down right this minute and enjoy yourself!"

By then the other guys on the truck were laughing themselves sick. In fact, in a few minutes we were all rolling around on the bags of rice laughing so hard I thought we were going to pop. By the time we got to Soe, that farmer was laughing the loudest of all of us. But I can tell you one thing for certain: he sure was relieved to let the truck take care of his stuff so he could sit back and enjoy the ride.

But you know, sometimes we're just as ridiculous. If God is

so great that He can design and create everything in this entire universe, and then He's smart enough to keep it in perfect working order so that nothing gets out of whack, surely taking care of our little problems won't be a bit hard for Him.

Do you know the reason we worry so much? I believe we don't really know what our wonderful God is like. Oh, if only we could realize how His great tender heart just aches for us when we're in trouble! If only we could realize how He longs to show us that He cares about us so much that He is willing even to share our sorrows. The Bible says that in all our trials and problems the Lord Jesus is right there suffering with us (Isaiah 63:9). He's actually going through the very same thing that we're going through—the same sorrow, the same frustration, the same disappointment or embarrassment. He's feeling it too, just like we are!

But the most wonderful thing of all is that His saving power and strength is right there with us to deliver us—to lead us out of our trouble. The Lord's loving Father-heart just yearns over us to draw us close to Himself where we can be safe and sheltered and happy in His love. When we're really trusting Him, when we're safely and securely resting in His bosom, it will be easy for Him to completely deliver us from our problems.

My friends, all we have to do—it's so simple that we often miss it—is to tell the Lord all about our problems and then just relax and leave it with Him. He's perfectly capable of doing the job Himself. In fact, when we've finally let go, He'll even do an exceeding-abundantly-beyond-all-that-we-ask-or-think kind of job for us! (Ephesians 3:20)

But now I'd like to tell you something else. I believe God's love goes a step beyond just the negative side of solving our problems for us. I believe He wants to positively shower us with all the blessings of both heaven and earth! Of course He wants to meet our *needs*; the Bible says that over and over again. (Just look at Matthew 6:25-32, Luke 12:30-32, and Philippians 4:19.)

But even more than that, I believe He wants to satisfy our desires, to give us lots of things (that maybe we can't honestly say we need) just to make us happy. Sometimes we get the screwy idea that God is stingy with His blessings. We can't work up enough nerve to ask Him for something unless we're sure we can adequately prove that it's a *need,* not a *want.*

Praise the Lord, that's a lot of nonsense. Our God delights in making us happy. Jesus is thrilled when we give Him the chance to meet the desires of our heart. He isn't picky about whether what we ask is a need or a want. As long as it's good for us, He's going to make sure that we get it.

That reminds me of something that happened to me once. Did I ever tell you about the time the Lord Jesus gave us a nice airplane ride? Well, my sister, brother-in-law, and I had been preaching in the island of Sumba for seven months. This was in 1967; by then the teams had started leaving Timor to witness for Jesus. We'd been working hard there, and it was time to go home.

That's when the Lord gave us a wonderful surprise. "Fin and Franz," He told my sister and brother-in-law, "I want you to leave Sumba on Monday, October 15. Mel will go on home a week later. But since you have been so faithful to Me, I'm going to arrange it so that you all get to go home by airplane."

Oh, boy, were we ever excited! This was a real treat. We thought we'd have to go home in a stinky boat as usual. Jesus was giving us the royal treatment. And I tell you, we felt as rich as kings—even though we didn't have one single rupiah to buy the airplane tickets.

The night of October 14 a man gave us enough money to pay for all three fares. So you see, we were rich after all. We had the key to the treasuries of the King of Kings. (Would you like to know where the man got the money he gave us? That's another story in itself. He'd been working in a government office for years, and often he would work overtime. But somehow the government never got around to paying him for those extra hours. I think the Lord must have given them a little kick in the seat of the pants, because the day before we were supposed to leave they finally paid the man the whole sum. He gave us one tenth of it as a tithe to the Lord, and it was just the amount we needed. You know, I believe that all those years the Lord had His thumb on that money. Those poor government guys couldn't have given it away even if they had wanted to; the Lord made them wait until we were there to get it.)

Happy and excited, we arrived in the airport early Monday morning. We still didn't have our reservations, because, as you know, we'd gotten our money at the last minute. But that didn't worry us a bit. Confidently I walked up to the ticket agent. "Sir, may I please have two seats on the airplane to Kupang today?"

I'm sorry," he announced in an important-sounding voice. "All the seats have been reserved."

"But what if there happen to be some extra ones?"

"If there are, then three army officers are going to take them." That was in an even more important-sounding voice, a little louder than necessary.

"But you know, it's possible there still might be some seats left. If there are, can I have two?"

"No, you can't!" (He said this way too loud; his dignity was beginning to slip a little bit.) "See those three Moslem priests over there? They're going on their holy pilgrimage to Mecca. They get next chance."

"But what if there just happens to be some more room?" I know I sounded like a stubborn mule, but if Jesus wanted to give us a nice airplane ride, I sure wasn't going to miss it!

Boy, that guy sure looked like he didn't like me too much. It seemed like he was thinking, *Oh, shut up and get out of here, you icky pest!* But instead he said, "Listen here, mister, if there's any place left, we're *not* sending you! Look out that window. See those big drums of oil? They need them in Kupang much worse than they need you. *And that's final!*"

When the airplane arrived there was enough weight allowance for three more people. So real quick the three army officers jumped on board. The three Moslem guys angrily walked out and went home.

The agent gave me a triumphant look. "See, mister, I told you so. *There's just plain no place for you!*"

But I wasn't going to let him discourage me. "I'm sorry, sir, but that's just not true. Jesus is my Master. And no matter what *you* might say, *He* told me that two of us are going today. I know that somehow He's going to get us on that plane!" Oh, that poor guy! He was too mad to talk, but he glared at me as if I were his eight-year-old son about to get a good spanking.

A few minutes before takeoff the worker who was counting the weight looked up at the ticket man. "I'm sorry, I made a mistake. There's enough weight allowance for one more person."

The agent poked his head into the waiting room. "Are the Moslem priests still here?" he called.

"No!" everybody shouted back. "They went home half an hour ago!"

The poor agent looked sort of sick to his stomach as he mumbled under his breath, "I guess one of you can go then."

My sister hopped on the scales with all her baggage. Before we knew it, the worker was saying, "Sorry! Another mistake! We still have room for one more."

That poor, poor agent! His face looked like a red overripe papaya ready to burst and squirt little black seeds (his angry words) all over the place. But before that could happen, my sister and brother-in-law hurried into the plane. Wow! Sometimes my Jesus goes to an awful lot of trouble just to make us happy.

He wants our lives to be rich and abundant: rich with close friends and lots of fun, rich with good health, rich with creative ways to use our talents. He even wants us to have good tasty food to eat, nice clothes to wear, and nice stuff to own that we'll really enjoy.

But above all He wants our lives to be rich and overflowing with the treasures of His love and His presence. And this is really the key. Because when we are utterly captivated by the Lord Jesus Himself, none of these things He gives us will pull us away from Him. Instead they will just make us realize more and more how utterly wonderful our Master really is. That's why the psalmist told us to delight ourselves in the Lord— because then He really will be able to give us all the desires of our heart! (Psalm 37:4)

I think it would be a good idea if we took some time out right now to have a Bible verse feast together. (While you're eating, let God's beautiful promise soak right through you, all the way down to your heart. Let His Word change your life and make you strong and healthy.)

Let's start with Psalm 81:10 for an appetizer. "Only test me! Open your mouth wide and see if I won't fill it. You will receive every blessing you can use!" (Living Bible) Now this verse hits me in just the right spot, because I have a big mouth. But see, it says I can never ask for or long for too much from my Jesus.

And look at Psalm 34:8-10 (from the Living Bible again). "Oh, put God to the test and see how kind he is! See for yourself the way his mercies shower down on all who trust in him. If you belong to the Lord, reverence him; for everyone who does this has everything he needs. Even strong young lions sometimes go hungry, but those of us who reverence the Lord will never lack any good thing." (Oh, isn't our God too precious for words? I just want to love and worship Him.)

Now let's have a scrumptious dessert from Psalm 68:19 (King James Version), "Blessed be the Lord, who daily loadeth us with benefits, even the God of our salvation." Wow! Did you notice that it says he *loads* us with benefits? He doesn't just give us some for a teaser. But He loads us with them until we can't carry anymore. And do you know what a benefit is? Well, that's very easy: it's anything that can possibly benefit us! Anything that can make us happier or stronger or more full of His abundant life.

And how often does He load us with these benefits? Every single day! Every single day, whether it's sunny or rainy, whether we have a stomach ache and stubbed our toe the first thing when we jumped out of bed, or whether we feel so healthy we could climb ten trees; whether we are terribly excited because our wife just had a cute little baby, or whether our hearts are grief-stricken because our best friend just died. Yes, every single day, no matter what, our loving heavenly Father wants to use both the joys and troubles of life to benefit us. My friend, let's open our minds and hearts wide to receive all the beautiful things He wants to give us. Let's never shut Him out by our fears or doubts about His love.

I know one thing for sure. Our Lord Jesus is far more generous than we could ever imagine. Why, if we only give Him the chance, do you know what He'll do? He'll fling open the floodgates of heaven, and He'll turn on all the blessing faucets at once, full force. And then He'll just drench us in His heavenly rainstorm. Pretty soon we'll be filled to the brim and overflowing with His blessings—the way we always wanted to be. Wow! Now that's what I call the abundant life!

Do you remember the story of "Peter and the Miraculous Draught of Fishes"? (I got that funny name out of a big Bible storybook.) Well, poor Peter had been working as hard as he could all night, but he didn't catch a single thing, not one single floppy, slithery fish!

Poor Peter. There he sat by the Sea of Galilee, his big shoulders sagging with discouragement, the sweat still dripping out of his reddish-brown beard. The net had slipped out of his calloused hands a long time ago. It lay there in a tangled, tattered mess on the sand. "Oh, what's the use anyhow?" Peter muttered through his teeth. "I might as well give up and become an unleavened-bread baker; at least they make some dough once in a while."

But who was that coming toward him? That lively, springing step looked familiar. And it seemed like he'd seen that flashy smile somewhere before. Oh, it was the new teacher from Nazareth.

"Hi, Peter. I was wondering if you could do me a favor. Pretty soon a huge crowd will be here, and I know from experience they'll almost squash me to death. I really need a boat to sit in while I preach. I was wondering if I could borrow yours. And can you help me push it out a little farther into the water?"

Peter stood up and stretched his aching muscles. "Sure, Teacher, anything you say."

Somehow, as he went sloshing through the water, the world didn't seem such an ugly shade of gray; things were beginning to look a little brighter. Half an hour later, as Peter sat there in his little boat lost in thought, his misery had completely disappeared, like fog in the bright morning sunshine.

Peter had never heard a sermon like this in his whole life! *What's this guy saying, anyway? How in the world can God be that nice to us? God wants to take care of us and help us? Boy, that kind of God sure sounds nice to me . . . . Hey! How did this guy ever find out so much about God? Sounds like He's His best friend. Who is this guy, anyway? I wonder where He ever came from? Boy, if I only had the chance, I'd sure like to ask—*

"Peter!"

"Huh?" Peter jumped off the upside-down fish crate he'd been sitting on as if it had an angry Roman soldier under it. "What! Oh. Oh, hi, Jesus. I—I guess You sort of scared me." Then a silly look crossed his face. "Oh, I guess the sermon was done ten minutes ago. But honest, Jesus, I was listening. I'm not kidding. I honestly wasn't daydreaming. I guess I was just—"

"Take it easy there, man!" Jesus couldn't help laughing at him. He looked so funny standing there with his face so red and screwed up, his hair sticking straight out all over his head, blowing around in the wind.

"Say, Peter, could you do me another little favor? I was wondering if we could go fishing right now. I know how you didn't catch a single thing last night—"

Peter gasped. *What! How in the world did He ever find out about that?*

"But if you'll try again right now, I promise you, the Lord will help you catch a whole lot of fish. He cares about you, you know, Peter."

Peter didn't know what to think. Anybody knew it was downright stupid to go fishing in broad daylight. But still . . . .

This guy said God cares about me! Me, Peter bar Jonah! Wow! And He sure sounds like He knows what He's talking about. Hey, who is this guy, anyway? I just can't stand not knowing! I wonder, I wonder if He could possibly be the Messiah. Maybe not, but at least there's a skinny chance . . . .

"Well, I'll tell you, Jesus. If I did it for anyone else I'd think I was a crazy nut ready to be shipped off to the Gadarenes. But somehow, to be honest, it seems like there's something really different about You. Anyway, I guess it can't hurt to try."

Jesus had a tender look in His eyes as He smiled at Peter . . . .

I wish you could have seen them twenty-five minutes later! They were up to their knees in slimy, flopping fish. The sweat was pouring off their hairy chests like water from an over-sopped sponge. Jesus had thrown off his red and yellow striped robe long ago; it lay somewhere over there in the corner under a pile of shiny fish.

And boy, was that net ever heavy! *R-r-rip.* "Oh, no! Not again! Quick, Andy! Get James and John! We need lots of help! Lots and lots of help—"

All of a sudden Peter stopped dead in his tracks.

'The Lord will help you catch a whole lot of fish.' He said that! I heard him say that! He was right! Jesus!

Peter couldn't control himself any longer. He didn't care if he smelled like fish for a month—his wife was used to it by now. He flopped down on his face, on top of all those fish, right there in front of Jesus.

"Oh, Lord Jesus! I know who You are now! You *are* the Messiah! You're my God, and You care about me! *Me, Peter!* Oh, Jesus, You're too wonderful! I—I just c-can't st-stand it!"

Peter was crying hard by now. He couldn't stop himself. He

knew he often acted way too emotional. Sometimes he even made James and Andrew squirm. But this time he just couldn't help it . . . .

And my friends, I know you'd act just as emotional if you came face-to-face with our wonderful God and found out just how much He cares about you. Enough to prove it by being terribly, terribly generous. Enough to prove it by loading your boat with a huge cash crop of fish!

I like to call all the wonderful things the Lord Jesus does for us His love-gifts to us. You know, He doesn't have to do such sweet things—He doesn't have to give and give to us, or solve our problems or satisfy our desires. No, they are extra little presents, little tokens of His love, that He delights to give us.

One of my best friends here in Soe told me about a love-gift the Lord gave her once. (Now actually, I shouldn't have said that last word *once*. Since the revival started, the Lord has given us these presents lots of times, hundreds and hundreds of times, in fact. But I don't have time to tell you about all of them.)

Well, on this particular day in January of 1971, a big, blustery storm was brewing in the sky. My friend Sus Ully (actually her real name is Julianna, but we like to give everybody nicknames) and four other friends, Tanta Tin, Pak Ataupah, Mamma Manao, and Mamma Tunliu, were in the little village of Noelaku, about ten miles from Soe. They were hoping they could get home before the storm actually boiled over. (Oh dear, I'm sorry I keep interrupting myself. But I think I'd better explain something else. In Indonesia, and especially in Soe, we all feel like we're in one big happy family. So we give everyone names like Auntie (*Tanta*), or Papa (*Pak*), or Big Sister *(Sus)*, or Big Brother *(Bu)*, or Little Brother *(Adik)*, or whatever else seems to describe the person pretty good. If you came to Soe to visit us and stayed around for a while, we'd think up a name for you too.)

But honestly, when Sus Ully looked at those huge black clouds, she didn't think they'd ever make it. It looked like those big guys were going to tip over any minute and start splashing gallons and gallons of rain down on all of them. And Sus Ully knew she sure didn't want that to happen!

"Oh Lord Jesus, please, please help us!" she cried.

(Now here comes the exciting part.) Right away the Lord spoke urgently in her heart. "Look up in the sky, over your head!" Sus Ully looked. And there in the sky, where a moment before there had been only angry storm clouds, was a big, beautiful angel, dressed in a white robe. And in his hands what do you think he was holding? Not a sword, but an umbrella!

"Now put both of your arms straight up over your head," the Lord went on, "and keep them there. As long as your arms are up, I won't let a drop of rain fall on any of you." By then all the mountains and trees around them were soaking wet. But not Sus Ully and the others; what the Lord had told her to do really worked. Even though Sus Ully was the only one who saw the vision of the angel, not one of them felt a drop of rain! In fact, everything within a three-hundred-foot radius stayed dry. As they were walking along, the dry circle moved forward with them.

Poor Sus Ully! Her shoulders started to get awfully tired. Whenever she'd put her arms down just a second to rest a little bit, the heavenly umbrella would real quick spring a leak; they'd all start to get wet. So as fast as she could she'd have to try to stick her arms up in the air again. (That reminds me of the story of Moses and the Amalekites in Exodus 17—except that poor Sus Ully didn't have any Aaron and Hur to help her!)

Well, they walked the ten miles back to Soe just praising the Lord for His mercies and sweetness. They finally reached Mamma Tunliu's house—it was the closest one. Just the split second that they were all safely through the door, God must have snapped His big umbrella shut, whisked it back into His heavenly coat closet, and slammed the door with a bang. Because, boy, that rain started pouring out of heaven, drenching the spot they'd been in just half a second before, as if the rainy season thought this was his last chance to live up to his name. When Sus Ully and all my other friends saw that, they told me that tears began rolling down their cheeks—tears of thanksgiving, tears of wonder that God would even be interested in protecting them from a storm.

I think I'd like to tell you one more story about the presents Jesus gives us. I think it's important for you to have a lot of examples so you'll be able to recognize them in your own life. You know, every day Jesus does wonderful, sweet little things for us. But often we're so blind we don't even notice them. Unless we realize that the blessings in our life come from Jesus' hand and that they are a special proof of His love for us, we'll miss most of the joy He wanted us to have.

This story happened the day after my brother-in-law and his team walked across the river that was thirty feet deep. I hope you remember that story from the book *Like a Mighty Wind.* Well, the whole reason they were in a hurry to cross the river and couldn't wait till the flood went down so they could walk on dry land was because the Lord had told them they *must* go as soon as possible to the village I want to tell you about. Its name is Bijaesahan. (Don't the Timorese people give their villages funny-sounding names?)

After a long walk the team finally reached the village, hungry and tired. But they found bad news waiting for them. The village was in the middle of a famine. The pastor with whom the Lord had told them to stay didn't have a bit of food in his whole house.

Of course the pastor wanted them to go someplace else where they could find some food. The most embarrassing thing he could think of was to have his guests stay in his house the three days the meetings lasted without giving them a single bite to eat the whole time. But my brother-in-law stood firm. He was going to obey the Lord by staying with the pastor even if it meant the whole team would have to suffer.

But I believe that my Jesus was watching them from His palace in heaven. It just blessed and thrilled His heart to pieces to see how His children wanted to honor Him and follow His leading no matter what it cost them. They had proved their love for Him. And like someone has said, "The Lord is no man's debtor." So the Lord Jesus decided that He was going to abundantly shower His love and mercy on the team by doing something for them that they had never before experienced in their whole life.

That night after the first meeting was over, the team came home terribly, terribly hungry. Then the Lord Jesus told my brother-in-law to gather the team, the pastor, and his family together for a prayer meeting. As my brother-in-law led out in prayer, a wonderful thing happened. The Lord gave every one of them there the same vision.

Some beautiful angels came down from heaven carrying a table. They spread it with a snowy white tablecloth—the Timorese people had never seen anything so pretty! And then do you know what those angels did? After setting the plates and spoons, they put a beautiful red rose beside each one's place. Jesus even wanted the table to look pretty for them.

And then came the food, bowl after bowl of it: rice, pork, chicken, vegetables, and some tea. When everything was ready, those having the vision saw themselves seated around the table, and they began to eat. Oh, I tell you, it was really a feast! The chefs in heaven had really prepared a masterpiece that time. It was so delicious that some of the people sitting in the room having the vision were actually smacking their lips out loud.

Finally when everyone had enough to eat and was full, my brother-in-law finished his prayer and said amen. (He'd been praying out loud the whole time.) Then everybody looked around at each other with a surprised look on their faces. They weren't hungry anymore. In fact, they were so full they could hardly move.

The Lord gave them this same vision every mealtime until the meetings were over. The food in the vision must have had a lot of vitamins and protein in it, because somehow it gave them enough energy to serve Him happily.

Now why would Jesus do a sweet thing like that? I believe He wanted to draw them all even closer to Himself so that He could just bathe them in His love. He knows that only by living close to His side, right next to His heart, will we ever find contentment and satisfaction in life. Only then will we know the joy and happiness God created us to experience.

3
Simple Faith

It was the first week I had ever been on a team. I stood there at the front of the little congregation with a spiritual look on my face. I felt pretty holy, because in a few minutes we were going to pray for the sick.

But then I saw him. Oh, *ugh!* That poor man! I felt like I was going to get sick and throw up any minute. His legs were like skinny, shriveled sticks hanging out of his body. But they didn't hang down straight either. Oh, no! They were so bent up and twisted out of shape that they looked more like pieces of broken pretzel than legs.

Of course he couldn't walk. He had to scoot along on his seat with those two ugly leg-things bumping and banging over the ground. He had taken coconut half-shells and made something like shoes for his hands so they wouldn't get cut up on all the sharp rocks lying around. But I guess he'd just given up trying to protect his legs because they were full of bruises and bloody welts.

This poor guy was waiting his turn in the healing line. But brother, you'd better believe me, by then all my holy feelings had disappeared. I sure didn't want to get stuck praying for him. It looked like a ridiculously impossible case to me.

So I chose the easier ones. First I prayed for a lady who

Simple Faith

couldn't breathe properly, and Jesus healed her right away. Then I prayed for someone with a stomach ache, and the Lord fixed him up too. Out of the corner of my eye I kept looking at that awful-looking man. *I wish one of those other team members would hurry up and pray for him,* I thought.

I prayed for about four other people. And finally—well, you can guess what happened. That guy was the last one in line, and the seven other team members were all busy. (They were probably thinking the same thing I was.) I just plain *had* to do the job. Jesus had me stuck in the corner really good that time.

As I walked over to the crippled man I was crying in my heart, "Oh, Lord, You've *got* to help me! Jesus, why did you ever get me into this mess! Get me out of here quick!"

I laid my hand on the guy, but I didn't know what in the world to say. I thought real hard and fast. Finally I decided to copy Peter. In a loud but quavery voice I plunged in: "Silver and gold have I none"—of course that didn't have anything to do with his problem—"but such as I have give I thee: In the name of Jesus Christ of Nazareth rise up and walk!" (Acts 3:6, KJV)

So far so good, I thought, but then Jesus whispered something in my ear. "Take him by the hands and lift him up; I want to heal him."

Boy, I tell you, that scared me stiff. If only Jesus hadn't said that. I could have patted that man on the back and said, "Well, brother, maybe your healing will be gradual," and walked away. But now I was in a jam worse than ever. The Lord was making me prove my faith. And at this point it was so terribly wavery that it seemed like it couldn't hold out another minute.

Well, I took a deep breath and grabbed that man by his skinny arms. I yanked and I pulled and he slowly tottered to his feet. Wow! He was horribly wobbly—almost as bad as my faith. I half-expected him to fall over with a thud.

But do you know what? He didn't. In just a few minutes his legs got stronger and stronger. Before I knew it he was taking a few steps all by himself. And then, praise the Lord, he

45

walked down the aisle and out the door! He must have gone home and eaten like a horse, because in a few days his legs were as fat and strong as mine are.

Wow! I really learned my lesson that time. I'd better never underestimate the Lord's power, because *nothing* is impossible for Him to do. And when He tells me He wants to do something, I had better cooperate.

Can you guess what I want to talk to you about now? If you're pretty smart, you've probably already figured it out from the title. Simple faith.

The Bible makes it obvious that it's pretty important. Jesus told that little lady with the issue of blood, "Daughter, your *faith* has made you well" (Luke 8:48). And to the two blind guys that were following Jesus begging to be healed He said, "Be it done to you according to your *faith*" (Matthew 9:29).

What did Jesus mean by that? Well, faith is like the gate of our heart that lets the Lord's power in. If the gate is open just a crack, then only a little bit of His power can squeeze through. If we really trust the Lord and are confident that all of His promises to us are going to come to pass, then our heart-gate is wide-open. God is free to do whatever He wants for us.

But—and this is the sad part—if we don't have any faith at all, the Lord Jesus just plain can't help us, no matter how badly He wants to. Do you know why? Because Jesus is a gentleman. He won't bang down the walls of our heart. He won't crash His way through into our lives if the gate is tightly shut against Him. He respects our human dignity and our free will too much to do that.

When I read through the pages of my New Testament I get the idea that lots of times Jesus was pretty sad when He lived on earth. I can just hear Him saying to His disciples, "Why do you guys keep doubting Me all the time? Why can't you believe in My power? Has there ever been a situation that was out of My control and too messy for Me to fix up?" (See Matthew 14:31;

16:8; Mark 4:40, and Luke 9:41.)

Do you know why it hurts the Lord's feelings when we don't have faith in Him? Maybe we don't really love Him with *all* our hearts or believe that He is going to keep His promises. Otherwise it would be easy for us to trust Him.

But there was at least one man in the Bible who had the kind of faith the Lord is looking for: faith that is simple enough to thrill and satisfy Jesus' heart. Faith that is simple enough to bring tremendous results. Do you know which man I'm talking about?

Gaius sat down on the little leather bench at the foot of his bed and reached for his writing table. Yes, he knew what had to be done. There was only one person who could help him now; and he was determined to get the whole matter settled as soon as possible.

But my! It had been a long night. Gaius' red soldier uniform was rumpled and dirty, and he could hardly keep his eyes open. His usually straight, broad shoulders were slumped over in exhaustion.

All night long, Marcus, his own beloved Marcus who was dearer to him than a brother, had been moaning in pain. Every once in a while he'd start to thrash around on his cot, kicking and rolling his eyes in the most terrifying manner. None of the government physicians could do anything to help. Marcus was dying of that dreaded tropical disease that no one could cure.

Gaius knew there wasn't much time left. He had to act quickly. But as he reached for his quill and a fresh parchment, he couldn't quite push away the thoughts that were swirling through his brain.

His mind raced back to his early days in Rome. When he was just a little boy his mother had brought him to the big temple on Via Veronica three times a week to offer meat sacrifices to her favorite gods—Jupiter, Diana, and Mars. But even then the whole thing was repulsive to Gaius. He could never believe that those stupid gods were really alive and at all interested in helping him out with anything.

As a young man he had decided to make the army his career. And because he was so hard-working, he had been promoted many times. Gaius enjoyed the army well enough. But somehow all his success could never drown out that emptiness he always felt in his heart.

He knew there had to be a real God, a loving God, somewhere in the universe. But how would he ever find Him? How could he know God personally? That question had haunted Gaius day and night for years.

It wasn't until he had been sent to the tiny province of Galilee a year ago to serve as a centurion that he felt like he was beginning to find the answer. He had been fascinated by the religion of the Jews. They claimed to belong to a God who was everything he had ever dreamed of—the all-powerful Creator of the world, the only one who was perfectly holy and righteous—just the opposite of those wicked Roman gods. And best of all, this most loving Father cared deeply about the needs of His children.

The Jews were very fanatic. They said they were God's chosen people and the only ones He was interested in. But Gaius could never make himself believe that that was true. Hadn't he been earnestly seeking for God all his life? And didn't he need God's love and power every bit as much as those Jews did?

Gaius had peace in his heart about one thing: he finally knew who the real God was. But yet that longing and emptiness was still there. What good did it do to know *about* God if He still wasn't your personal friend? Gaius wanted to experience God for himself. He wouldn't be content until God had revealed Himself to him.

After hours of turning this problem over in his mind, he finally realized he was longing for the very same thing that many of his Jewish friends were. He was longing to meet the Messiah—the God-man who would come to earth to live with His people.

But suddenly everything was changed! Just a week ago Gaius' whole world had sprung to life. Now vibrancy and joy were surging through his being. Gone was that aching emptiness. And in its place, way down in his heart, was a beautiful glowing, excited feeling that Gaius just couldn't explain. All he knew was that it seemed like he had been resurrected. Real, true life was right there waiting for him with open arms.

He remembered the morning it had all happened. He had been off duty and had strolled down to the lakeshore to see what was attracting such huge crowds. That was when he had his first glimpse of *Him*—the one he had been seeking all his life. *He* was on earth now! O wonder of wonders, the Messiah was finally here!

Gaius knew Him the second he laid eyes on Him. He didn't have any doubts—this Jesus of Nazareth was no mere man. He was God! Why, the very image of God was stamped across His personality. Those beautiful words He said, "The Spirit of the Lord . . . has sent Me to proclaim release to the captives, and recovery of sight to the blind, to set free those who are downtrodden," and those tremendous miracles of healing were all the proof Gaius needed.

And now, as he sat at his writing table, a smile slowly spread across his face. To anyone else the situation would look desperate—his most beloved servant struck down two days ago with that dreadful palsy, dying an agonizing death. Before he met Jesus, Gaius would have been panic-stricken. But now he knew there was no reason to be afraid. Wasn't it the very nature of God to love and heal and save people with His wonderful power?

He had no time to lose however. Quickly he scratched out a message on the parchment, rolled it into a scroll, and sealed it with his special stamp. He clapped his hands loudly, and instantly a soldier appeared in the doorway.

"Here," ordered Gaius. "Take this scroll down to the fisherman's hut by the lakeside. See that it gets into the hands of Jesus of Nazareth. Now hurry!"

Just half an hour later the soldier had pushed his way through the crowd and was standing at Jesus' side.

Jesus carefully unrolled the scroll.

Most Honorable Rabbi Jesus,

I humbly request you to heal my beloved servant, Marcus, who is dying of palsy. I know no one else has power to heal him. Only You do, because You are God.

It is not necessary for You to come to my house. You have all authority to heal him right where You are. If You just speak a word, I know he will be restored to health. Thank You for Your compassion and willingness to help.

Respectfully and gratefully Yours,
Centurion Gaius Tertius

Jesus looked up from the scroll. His lips were parted in a radiant smile, and His eyes began to sparkle and shine with all the light of glory. His resonant voice vibrated with joy as He said, "I have never before found anyone with such simple faith as this. No, not even among the chosen people of Israel!"

And of course I don't even have to tell you that Gaius received just what he asked for: Marcus was completely healed that very hour. Yes, Jesus had proved beyond a shadow of a doubt that He was truly the Son of God.

Now Gaius had simple faith. But how can we have it? How can we have that same kind of faith that brings so much honor to the Lord Jesus and brings such fantastic results for ourselves? Well, first of all, before we can start to practice it, I think we have to know what simple faith really is.

Can I tell you a little definition that has been really useful to me over the years? Simple faith is nothing more than a natural result of *knowing Jesus,* of being close enough to Him to know what He wants to do in a certain situation—and then simply doing whatever He tells us to do to help Him.

Did you notice how Gaius did all of this exactly right? Praise the Lord that the Holy Spirit decided to put him in the Bible. He's a perfect laboratory specimen for us to examine. If you don't mind, let's stick Gaius under the spiritual microscope and see what we can learn from him.

Well, number one, Gaius really knew Jesus. He knew that Jesus was *God*. And if He was God, then it was simple to figure out that He had the *power* to heal Marcus. (Now the same thing is true for us—we can't hang around the Lord Jesus very long before we'll find out that He has a fantastic, stupendous power—the power to do anything we ask Him to do, and the power to do a whole bunch of other things that are far, far too wonderful for us even to imagine.)

But Gaius knew something else about Jesus, too. He knew that Jesus not only had the *power* but also the *love* to heal Marcus. He could see straight through to the depths of Jesus' tender heart. He could see all the compassion and warm tenderness that was beating out this message: *"I love you, Gaius! I care about you, Gaius! I yearn to meet your needs and do all that your heart desires!"*

Yes, Gaius knew that Jesus loved him, and that the Lord's deepest desire was to give him all he asked for. Oh, my friend, how you and I need to know that today! How we need to realize that Jesus cares about each one of us personally!

Just for one minute, pretend that you are the only person in the whole world, and that you are the only person God cares about. All day long He thinks loving tender thoughts about you and plans new ways to meet your desires. As far as God is concerned, all the promises in the Bible were written just for you, and you are the Lord Jesus' pride and joy. He loves you with a love that is so passionate and mighty that nothing, absolutely nothing is too great or too small for Him to do in your behalf.

My friend, this is an accurate picture; it is not exaggerated. God loves you exactly this way. He is so great and infinite that He can and does love you as if you're the only person in the world. His fantastic love is that personal! Praise the Lord!

Now this fact ought to get the wheels in your brain turning *wow!* I hope you're thinking, *Then this means that God wants to help me. Plain old ordinary little* me! *I don't care how many other guys He's used His power on, He wants to use it on me! Boy, I'm sure not going to let His power and love lie around in heaven all day doing nothing except getting rusty. I'm going to ask God to make it get to work to help* me!

Now Gaius had this attitude. And because of that He was able to do part two of simple faith real well. (In case you've already forgotten our definition of simple faith, I'll read you part two: "being close enough to Jesus to know what He wants to do in a certain situation.")

Gaius simply put two and two together and got four. *God has enough power to heal Marcus* plus *God loves and cares enough to heal Marcus* equals *God wants to heal Marcus.* And once Gaius knew that God *wanted* to heal Marcus, why, it was just a matter of common sense to realize that He *was going to heal Marcus!*

To Gaius it was obvious what Jesus wanted to do and was going to do in his particular situation.

This is the whole exciting secret of simple faith: knowing ahead of time what God is going to do. This is what makes simple faith so simple. But I'm going to whet your curiosity a little bit. I'm not going to tell you any more about part two right now (there are several things I still need to explain to you about it). Instead, let's go on to part three: "simply doing whatever He tells us to do to help Him."

If you wanted to, you could call this part *simple obedience.* (That's what I usually end up calling it myself.) Once you know what the Lord is going to do to fix up your problem, usually He will tell you to do something for Him first. You have to obey Him and do what He asks before His power will be set free to go to work.

Gaius knew He had to write a letter to Jesus asking Him to heal his servant before Marcus could ever be healed. Do you remember the story about the crippled guy that I told you at the beginning of this chapter? Well, I had to practice simple obedience by yanking that little old man to his feet. If I hadn't obeyed the Lord and done that, wow! To this day that poor guy would probably be scooting along on his seat with his ugly legs bumping and banging around on the ground.

Someday you might ask Jesus to do something for you. (But if there is some need in your life that is staring you in the face as you read these pages today, then I strongly encourage you to bring that problem to Jesus right now and ask Him to get to work on it.) If you ask Jesus to heal your body, He may tell you to call your Sunday School teacher on the phone and ask him to pray for you. Then He'll heal you. Well, in that case, just plain do what the Lord told you to do. Call your teacher on the phone. And you can be sure that the Lord *will* heal you just like He promised.

And let's say that you ask the Lord to save your daughter who has run away from home and is on drugs. Well, Jesus might tell you that you need to apologize to her for antagonizing her by something you've done. And He might say that you first need to be a real friend to her by spending hours listening to her problems (without preaching at her!) before He'll be able to save her. My friend, if the Lord ever tells you to do something like this, I urge you, please do it! Just obey Him step by step, following each thing He tells you to do. And pretty soon a beautiful miracle will be your reward.

Here's a little equation for you to remember:

$$\frac{\begin{array}{l} \text{simple faith (in God's power and love)} \\ +\quad \text{simple obedience (to God's commands)} \end{array}}{\text{a tremendous miracle!}}$$

Okay, now let's go back and pick up the part we skipped before. Remember? I was going to tell you some more about part two—the real crux of simple faith— knowing what God is going to do ahead of time, even before He does it.

Let's go back to our laboratory and stare at Gaius again under the microscope. We've already noticed that He really did know *what* Jesus was going to do; he knew Jesus was going to heal his servant.

But Gaius was even spiritually smarter than that. He actually knew *how* and *when* Jesus was going to heal Marcus. If you really examine those Bible verses in Matthew 8:5-13 and Luke 7:1-10, you will find that he knew both the *how* (by speaking just a word)—and the *when* (immediately). And sure enough, it happened exactly like he knew it would.

This is the real beauty of simple faith. It always brings 100 percent results. Did you notice that Gaius didn't have to do any guessing about what God's exact will was? And he didn't have to "screw up his faith" either. It wasn't a bit hard for him to trust the Lord to do what he was already positive the Lord was going to do.

There's a real nice verse in the Bible that I'm sure Gaius would have underlined and starred if it had only been written when he was alive. It says that if we can only find out what God's will about a particular problem is, and then we ask Him to solve it the way we already know He wants to, then we can be positive He'll do it just that way. (This is the Mel Tari version of that verse. In case you don't trust me and you'd rather look it up and read it in your own Bible, you can find it in 1 John 5:14,15.)

Here is the tricky part of simple faith: knowing the Lord so well and closely that you are able to tell exactly how and when He wants to do a miracle. My friend, I'm going to be dead honest with you. There are no shortcuts to this. There are no shortcuts to really knowing Jesus so well that we can even read His mind.

The only way we'll ever be able to know exactly what the Lord Jesus is thinking is by spending lots and lots of time with Him, by living in His presence every single minute. We'll have to be ready and listening when He starts to tell us the secrets of His heart. Believe me, our telephone lines to heaven are going to have to be awfully clear. Our ears will have to be tuned in to hear His faintest whisper in our hearts.

One thing that we'd sure better remember is that God is sovereign. We'd better not try to boss Him around. He has infinite wisdom and knows much better than we do what is best for us. We might have some spectacularly brilliant ideas (that's our own opinion, of course) about how and when He should do a miracle. But brother, we'd just better not try to boss God around or "claim by faith" that He'll do what *we* think is best, or else we're going to get in terrible trouble for sure.

Sometimes we might think that God is pretty stupid. We might think that He passes up an awful lot of golden opportunities to do some spectacular miracles. But praise the Lord, He has more sense than we do.

If we were God we would probably heal every sick guy in the hospital. (But the Lord knows that most of those guys need to have their souls healed and made right with Him first.) And maybe we'd try to show off our supernatural power by raising a whole bunch of dead guys back to life. (But God knows that a dramatic miracle like that can make us human beings take our eyes off Him and get so excited about the miracle that we forget all about Him. That's one of the worst things that could ever happen to us.)

I can tell you one thing for sure: since the revival started we've had to learn that we'd better not try to cheat God out of His job. We'd better not demand that He do something our way, just because we think we're so smart. We'd better never step out "in faith" that the Lord will do something unless He's clearly told us that He wants to do it that way.

Otherwise we'd have a big, terrible mess. If we tried to walk across a river that was thirty feet deep, for example, and the Lord hadn't told us to, even if we thought we had a terribly spiritual motive like witnessing to the Moslems who were standing on the banks watching, we'd all sink to the bottom of the river and be drowned for sure.

Some friends of mine made the mistake of claiming by faith that God would raise one of their friends from the dead without ever stopping to find out how God felt about the subject. They were so excited about their great idea. They kept telling God that if He'd only do this miracle He could bring lots of glory to His name and maybe even start a revival in their area.

But you and I should know that God does not have to defend Himself. *He does not have to do a miracle to prove that He is God.* The Lord never raised their dead friend back to life, probably because He knew the miracle would end up getting the glory instead of Himself.

Maybe He also knew that my friends would try to snitch a little bit of the glory too. They weren't strong enough yet to place all the credit solely at the feet of Jesus. If someone came up to them and said, "My, are you ever spiritual! Tell me, what is the secret of your great faith?" they'd let those flattering words go to their head and be spiritually ruined.

One time I made a big mistake myself. I got my own smart ideas all mixed up with God's will. I never really bothered to let Him tell me what *He* wanted to do, because I was so dead stuck on what *I*, Mel Tari, wanted.

But let me tell you what happened. One day when I was just a little boy I was taking a bath in the river. Now if you were a little kid living in Timor, that would be one of your favorite things to do—take a bath and jump and shout and splash around in the river.

My brothers and sisters and I used to chase each other down the steep banks, pull off all our clothes (no one else was looking and it was only us, so it really didn't matter), and jump into the icy mountain water. I'm not too sure how clean we got. But I know we'd wiggle around and squeal and scream and have an awful lot of fun.

Well, on this particular day I splashed around a little bit too much; I got water inside my ear. Now usually that would be a very minor problem. But somehow this time it caused a terrible infection. For years after that my ear hurt so bad that it would drive me half-crazy every so often. Every day some icky white stuff would ooze out of it, and oh, it smelled just awful.

One day in 1965, soon after the revival started in our big church in Soe, I went to a special meeting. A man named Nahor was praying for people to be healed. Even though this was a brand-new truth for us, I believed that what the Bible and the man said was true: God has power to heal *today*, and if we only have faith when we ask Him to heal us, He will.

Yes, this is for me, I thought. *I can't stand to have my ear drive me nuts one more day. Boy, I'm really glad I came to this meeting.* When the guy asked who wanted to be healed, I raised my hand along with the others.

"Okay, Jesus," I said in my heart, "please get busy. Please heal me now. Oh, hurry up, Lord, because I just can't wait. I know You've got to do what I ask You to because I have faith in my heart." All kinds of people all around me were getting healed instantly. They were very happy and excited. But nothing happened to me. I gave my faith a little poke in the ribs and told it to work harder. But still nothing happened. What in the world was wrong? Something had obviously gotten screwed up somewhere along the line.

Well, to make a long story short, that night I went home with the pain in my ear as strong as ever. It still felt like it was pounding nails through my head.

Oh well, maybe the Lord wasn't in the mood to heal me tonight, I told myself. *I guess I can stick it out one more day.* But the next day nothing happened either. Or the next. Or the next.

Several months later I was still waiting. I was tugging at Jesus' sleeve quite often to ask Him what in the world was the matter. Do you know, I had to wait two whole years before the Lord finally answered my prayer and healed my ear.

But during that time I learned a very valuable lesson. I had to learn to stop seeking the Lord for healing and seek Him for Himself alone. I had to learn that I needed Jesus much, much worse than I needed my ear to be healed.

You know, my friends, when the Lord doesn't answer our prayers the way we want Him to, it's a good sign that it's time for us to take our eyes off ourselves and our own desires and turn them only upon Him. We'd better draw just as close to Him as we possibly can so we'll be in a better position to hear His voice next time.

I've already told you about a flop I experienced. But now I'd like to show you a few cases where simple faith really worked; where someone knew ahead of time what the Lord was going to do, and it happened just exactly the way they knew it would. Oh, it just thrills me to see how real true simple faith always brings 100 percent accurate results.

Do you remember my friend Sus Ully whom I told you about in the last chapter? (In case you've been wondering, you are supposed to pronounce her name *YOU-lee.*) Well, she has another beautiful story to tell us.

I really wish you could have the chance to meet her sometime. She is such a sweet and precious sister. The Lord has continually been using her in a tremendous way ever since the revival started—probably because she is so obedient and trusts Him like a little child. Let's listen while she tells us what happened.

In 1971 an old lady from Soe that we call Nene Maria got very, very sick. Her friends got quite alarmed. They sent word to a man named Mr. Sarjito, asking him to come and pray for her. He asked me to go along with him to help.

By the time we got to Nene Maria's house, she had died. In fact, she had already been dead for six hours and her body was stiff and cold.

But immediately, just as soon as we stepped in the door, the power of the Holy Spirit came on me so strongly that I knew the Lord was going to do a wonderful miracle. He told me to rush over to the dead lady, lay my hands on her head, and start to pray.

Mr. Sarjito and I had been praying a few minutes when all at once the Lord Jesus gave me a beautiful vision. I saw myself in heaven before the throne of God. All around were beautiful angels, and on the throne sat the Lord Jesus Christ Himself, so glorious and full of love.

Then He spoke to me, "My child, you must go back to earth again." The angels picked me up, and with their strong rushing wings we flew down, down, down . . . "Oh, praise the Lord, praise the Lord!" I said, "Jesus is bringing her back!"

All of a sudden, before any of us knew what was happening Maria sat straight up in bed. She grabbed Mr. Sarjito by the knees. He was startled and scared half to death! She sat there smiling at us for a moment, her face radiant and glowing. Then she climbed off the bed and walked out to the bathroom in the back of the house.

When she came back, she told us an amazing story. She said she had been in heaven and had seen the most beautiful big buildings made of solid gold. They were far more beautiful than anything she had ever seen in Timor. She had talked with Jesus for quite a while, several hours perhaps, but to her it seemed like just a few minutes.

Jesus, wearing a long, white flowing robe, had looked at her and asked, "What is your name?"

"Maria," she answered Him.

"And how old are you?"

"I don't know, I can't remember."

Jesus opened His big book and looked through it. Then He spoke: "Yes, Maria, your name is written here in My Book of Life. And it says that you are seventy years old now."

After a while He told her it was time for her to go back to earth. He then commanded the two guards who stood by the gate of heaven to take her back. She and the angels had walked back to earth together, and now here she was.

By this time everybody in the room was worshiping and praising God. We all started to sing songs of joyful thanksgiving to Him. But we weren't actually surprised that Nene Maria had been raised from the dead. While we had been praying, we had felt the Lord Jesus' presence so strongly. And since the Lord of life Himself was in our midst, it was no problem at all to believe that He'd bring us the resurrection and life He had promised.

And you know, my friends, when our glorious Lord Jesus is

with us, miracles seem like the most natural thing in the world to happen.

One night in July of 1973 my friend Tanta Ete was sound asleep in bed. She had been working hard at a young people's Bible camp we were having in the island of Alor. But all at once she began to have a strange and terrifying dream. She saw a crazy, mentally sick woman lunge at her, trying to attack. Her face was as ferocious and dangerous as a wild animal's—her eyes were bulging out and she was sticking her long tongue way out like a monkey.

But almost immediately in her dream Tanta Ete began to sing, "In the name of Jesus, in the name of Jesus, we have the victory!" (That's been one of our favorite songs ever since the revival started.) She sang and sang until pretty soon she woke up and found herself singing out loud!

"Oh, Lord," she began to pray, "how I praise You. You were right there with me the whole time so I could fight. And Lord, You really did give me the victory! I can just feel it so strongly in my heart. Oh, how I praise You that You have all power over the evil one."

Two days later the camp director asked Tanta Ete to lead a team of campers to the village of Watatuku. There was a demon-possessed lady there who needed the Lord's help very badly, and the campers wanted to minister to her.

When they were quite close to the woman's house, they all kneeled down to pray, asking the Lord for wisdom and guidance. But right away they heard a horrible, unearthly voice. Someone not far away was screaming and crying out and saying the most filthy, evil things imaginable. Then the team realized it was the woman they wanted the Lord to help. Although she still hadn't seen them, the demons inside of her knew the team was coming to cast them out. And they were determined not to leave without a real fight.

But instead of getting panicky and going back home because the situation was much, much worse than they thought it would be, those precious people began to worship the Lord. "We praise You, Lord, that You're right here with us with all Your wonderful power. In Your name no power of Satan or hell can stand against us." Oh, they felt such victory and excitement in their hearts. They couldn't wait to see what the Lord Jesus was going to do.

Then the Lord told Tanta Ete to open her Bible to 1 John 4:4. "You are from God, little children, and have overcome them," she read, "because greater is He who is in you than he who is in the world."

"Now this verse is our sword," she told the others. "The Lord Jesus Christ is right here with us. We will go into battle and we will win! His victory is ours. Come on, everybody, let's go!"

In a moment they saw the woman in her front yard, raging like a wild animal. Her sons had made her kneel on a board while they laid another heavy board on top of her legs, sort of like a sandwich. Then they nailed those boards together securely so the lady couldn't move. She was far, far too dangerous to be let loose.

All at once, without anyone leading them, the team members began to clap their hands and sing "In the Name of Jesus." The lady saw them coming. She picked up jagged rocks lying around her and snarled like a lion. "You come! You come! I'm going to throw these!"

But instead of getting scared, the team kept walking toward her. The wilder and more ferocious she got, the harder they sang. Finally, when they were just a yard away, the team made a circle around her, still praising the Lord and singing. Suddenly, wonder of wonders, she dropped all the sharp rocks she was planning to throw, bowed her head, and grew still.

Then in a gentle, quiet voice Tanta Ete began to talk to her. "In the name of Jesus I tell you that we are the servants of the Lord Jesus Christ. He loves you very much."

"Oh, no!" The demons couldn't stand to hear that; they started snarling again. "Oh, no! Oh, no, He doesn't!"

Tanta Ete: In the name of Jesus tell me who you are.

Demon: My name is Liliana Selsilia.

Tanta Ete: Oh, Liliana Selsilia, Jesus loves you so much.

Demon: Oh, no! I don't like that! Don't tell me that!

Then one of the team members whispered, "Oh, Tanta Ete, you made a horrible mistake. That's the demon's name. The lady's real name is Susana."

Tanta Ete: Okay, then, in the name of Jesus I command you to tell me who is Liliana Selsilia?

Demon: I have been walking around the world. I'm from America. I'm from Australia. I'm from Arabia, and Hong Kong, and Japan.

Tanta Ete: In Jesus' name tell me how many of you there are. (Tanta Ete knew that when we use the name of Jesus, Satan must answer. He has no choice, because Jesus is his Master.)

Demon: Four. There are four of us. I also come from Timor.

Tanta Ete: In the name of Jesus I command you to tell me: Where did you live in Timor?

Demon: Fatu Leu. (This is a huge rock near Camplong. It is a terrible stronghold of demonic power. Tanta Ete realized that after the revival started, some Christians had probably cast those demons out of Timor. They had wandered around the world to all of those other countries until they finally found a resting place in that poor woman in Alor. My friend, the power of evil is so thick in the air these last days. That's why it's so very important that at all times we live covered by the precious blood of Jesus, so that Satan can't get in to harm us.)

Tanta Ete: Do you know the name of Jesus?

Demon: No! No, we don't know that name; we know many gods, but not the name you said.

Tanta Ete: In the name of Jesus open your mouth and stick out your tongue.

As the lady obeyed, Tanta Ete and all the other team members began to pray out loud, "Oh, Lord, make this tongue confess your name."

Then a wonderful thing happened. In a clear voice Susana

said, "I want to sing a song." And she began to sing *"Jesus Cinta Saya"* ("Jesus Loves Me"). By then more than a hundred people from the village had gathered around. And like a huge joyful choir they all joined her in the song.

Immediately after the song was finished, Tanta Ete said, "You demons, tell me who you are."

Demon: Monkey. We are many monkeys.

Tanta Ete and team: You spirit of monkey, in the name of Jesus you must go out! Susana belongs to Jesus, not to you. (Praise the Lord, that demon was cast out of her right away. And in the same way they cast out the other three—deer, crocodile, and finally Liliana Selsilia.)

Oh, it was such a beautiful sight to see that dear woman set free by the power of Jesus' love and authority. Her face relaxed into a peaceful smile. And her eyes that were once so wild and wicked-looking grew tender.

Then she lifted her voice and led those hundred people in more than twenty different Christian songs. Her voice that was once so powerful in cursing for the devil was now strong and melodious in praising and adoring our precious Lord Jesus.

When she sang the song, "Out of my bondage, sorrow, and night, Jesus, I come to Thee," she almost started to cry. She was just overwhelmed with the joy of knowing she was secure in Jesus' mighty arms. No power of evil would ever be able to snatch her away from Him again. Ahead of her stretched a glorious and shining road where she would walk hand in hand with her Master, set free and filled by His love.

4
Romance with the King of Kings

The little hut huddled on the top of the mountain, shivering in the coolness of the night air. Whispering winds wrapped themselves around its walls like a cloak and tussled their fingers through its long, grasslike hair. Like guardian angels, the tall bamboo trees stood silently around the house, their leafy wings shimmering in the softness of the starlight. They gazed out across the peace of the mountainside, and down, down into the valleys where the shadows lay on the land like a blanket. The night was cradling the whole world in her arms, soothing it into a deep, dreamless sleep.

Inside the little hut, I knelt by the side of my wooden cot to say a final good-night to my Master. But suddenly, with no warning at all, the stillness of the night was shattered. Like a clear-toned bell His voice came ringing through the darkness; the sound reverberated in my ears.

"Mel, My son," the Lord was speaking to me, "I am giving you a new name. From now on I will call you David!"

With my face on the dirt floor, I knelt there stunned. By now my little room was glowing. A heavenly light brighter than a thousand floodlights was streaming through the grass roof. I knew that Jesus Himself was there. I felt Him wrapping His warm love around me. He was drawing me so close to His heart, to that place of perfect security and love, that I tingled in the depths of my being.

But what did His words mean? Why did He want to give me a new name? And why David? I just didn't understand . . . .

I waited. And then in the breathless hush His words of tenderness rose up in my heart. "My son, long before you were even born, I chose you to be My very own. I set My love upon you and gave you a special place in My Kingdom. In My love I have called you by your name.

"David was a man after my own heart. He lived close to me, and I was able to give him My rich treasures. I could pour out on him all the abundance of My kindness. I long for you to live close to Me too. I want to be your most cherished possession.

"As I promised King David, so I promise you. As long as the moon and stars hang glowing in the sky, I will love you and protect you. And all My many promises to you will never fail . . . ."

Jesus chose a very dramatic way to show me I was special to Him. But He longs for you just as much. I don't care who you are, even if you never had a real dramatic experience like I did, *you* are just as special and precious to Jesus. You might think you're a nobody or feel terribly unimportant. You might think God is so busy taking care of all the spiritual guys like the pastors and church elders that He doesn't have any time left over even to notice you. But that's not true!

Sometimes we get ourselves into a horrible mess. We get the funniest ideas about what God's love means. If we shut our eyes and screw up our face we can sort of picture Jesus sitting up in heaven on His throne. He's patting Himself on the back with a smug look on His face. "Aren't I wonderful to love such little rotten nobodies! What a bunch of worthless sinners! If it weren't for My wonderful grace, wow! They'd all be sizzling in hell for sure."

Oh, my friend, let's not spiritualize God's love. It's surely not love to think someone is repulsive, but then to grit your teeth and make yourself act loving to him anyway. Boy, I tell you, if God felt that way about me, it would hurt my feelings so bad that I wouldn't want to have anything to do with Him.

Let me tell you what real true love means. If the Bible says God loves you, it means He thinks you're wonderful and precious. It means He wants you and desires you very badly because you're so valuable to Him. It means He's ready to pay whatever price necessary to set you free from anything that's ruining your wonderful qualities.

That's the whole reason Jesus died for us; He saw tremendous potential in us. Some people I know go around saying.

"Man is basically *bad*. We are worthless sinners. There is no reason God should love us." Oh, that makes me feel sad; I just can't agree with them. Of course, it's true that we are sinners and our sin is very bad. But even before we sinned we were made in the image of God. And when God looked at us after His big creation job was over, do you know what His opinion of us was? "God saw all that He had made, and behold, it was very good" (Genesis 1:31). So according to God, you and I, at the very basic bottom are *very good*!

God made us in His own image; now that's a powerful statement. We were made to reflect His personality in all its glory and beauty. We were made in such a way that we could satisfy God's longing for human friendship and companionship. Believe me, that's a big honor!

God lavished the peak of His skill and creative genius on us in order to form us into a masterpiece that would delight His heart. And we do delight His heart. The Lord sees real beauty and value in our human personality. So He has every reason in the universe to love us. We *are* worthy of His love, not because of anything we *do* to try to make ourselves worthy, but simply because of who we *are*—His magnificent creation.

You and I are invaluable to God. That's why it made Him terribly, terribly angry to watch our sin and the devil send us to hell as if we were a bunch of garbage. That's why He gave His life to redeem us.

Do you know what it means to be redeemed? Well, when the Lord redeems us He helps us to escape from the ugly, coal-black shell of sin that was distorting our personality. He transforms us into a sparkling, glowing diamond that is worth millions upon millions of dollars. He creates us once again in His own beautiful image. Wow! Isn't the Lord's love for us fantastic!

You know, as long as we're focusing our eyes on our ugly shell instead of on the Lord's marvelous redeeming grace, we're never going to be able to enjoy God's love. When we condemn ourselves and wallow in guilt about our sin, the Lord's grace can never transform us. We're actually shutting God's love out of our hearts. And, oh, how the Lord Jesus longs for us to get thrilled to pieces over His love.

I think that when He was on earth, one of His favorite things to do was to show people they didn't have to feel condemned about their sin. In His love they were not only forgiven but also made perfect and beautiful. His love set them free to become the masterpiece God had created them to be.

Early one morning Jesus was in the Temple teaching. Suddenly a fierce mob of men burst into the courtyard. High above their heads they gripped a sobbing woman. Then with a mighty heave, they flung her into the dust at Jesus' feet.

A wicked sneer curled at the corners of their lips as they spat out, "Hah! Master. Now we've got you! See this ugly wretch? We caught her in the very act of adultery. The licentious beast! What do You say—she ought to be stoned to death, shouldn't she?"

One of them gave her a sharp kick in the ribs. Several others heaped the jagged rocks that littered the courtyard into big piles. Like a pack of bloodthirsty wolves they were ready to kill and devour.

There she lay in a terrified heap, face down in the dirt. Her whole body was shaking violently by now. The sweat and tears and saliva dripping off her face had formed muddy pools on the ground.

And Jesus? The Master was angry. Without a word He strode forward till He reached those murderous men. Then He stopped, towering above them like a mighty pillar of strength. Fire flashed from His eyes, and His lips were a thin hard line. But He didn't speak.

Silently He stared into their flushed faces. Never once did His gaze waver. His eyes had become two burning coals that pierced their way through into the deepest secrets of those men's hearts. His eyes were brilliant searchlights; without pity they exposed every evil motive, every greedy ambition, every filthy thought and desire. The men had nowhere to hide—nothing could escape the notice of those eyes.

The atmosphere of the courtyard was tense and breathless. Not a person moved. It seemed as if they had been transported to the very judgment hall of heaven. They were awaiting the verdict from the lips of the great Judge Himself.

Then with all the authority of almighty God, Jesus spoke: "He who is without sin among you, let him be the first to throw a stone at her."

His words flung themselves into the air and echoed off the walls of the Temple. The spell had been broken. One by one, their faces dark with shame, the men slunk off into the shadows.

Suddenly a peace filled the air and everything became very still. Jesus gazed tenderly at the woman. How much she had suffered that day! His eyes were filled with compassion as He slowly stooped and laid His hand on her head.

The woman looked up. Amazement was written across every line of her face. Why did this Man smile at her so warmly? Who was this Man who cared about her? Why had He touched her so gently? She had been touched before by men, many times. But they had only abused her. No one before had ever treated her with respect. Jesus took the woman by her shoulders and carefully lifted her to her feet. With the corner of His robe He wiped the tears off her face. His voice was soft as He asked, "Woman, where are they? Did no one condemn you?"

She stared around at the empty courtyard. A wild, astonished look leaped into her eyes. Every one of them was gone! And *He* had done it! He had not only defended her, but better yet, He had actually gotten rid of every one of her tormenters!

"Oh, Lord," she cried. "Not a single one of them is here to condemn me!"

Never before had she seen anyone look so majestic and beautiful. Never before had she felt such warm, vibrant love as when her Lord answered her, "My daughter, I will never, ever condemn you either. Because of My love you are free to go and sin no more."

Yes, Jesus can look deep into your heart and see what perhaps no one else can see—*the real, beautiful you.* He's just thrilled and delighted with you. The Bible even says so in plain English: "The Lord delights in you and will claim you as his own" (Isaiah 62:4, Living Bible).

Do you know what it means to have the Lord Jesus claim you? Well, for one thing it means that you're His prized possession, a beautiful treasure to Him. He can appreciate all those wonderful qualities about you that other people take for granted or maybe don't even notice. Jesus not only loves you, but He likes you—more than anyone in the world will ever like you.

But do you know what else it means to be claimed by Jesus? He actually longs for you. It is very important to Him that you and He be close friends with each other. Even if everyone else in the world was close to Him, He would still want you.

The Lord's love isn't cold and one-sided. Of course He loves to give to you, but He never wants to make you feel miserable by doing *all* the giving. This is what gives you your dignity as a human being: the heavenly Father and the Lord Jesus want to *receive* from you too. They know that in your relationship with them you are just as important as they are. You have an awful lot to contribute. And the amazing part of the whole thing is that what you do or don't do actually makes a difference to them.

When you whisper little I-love-you's to the Lord during the day, I can just imagine that His eyes start to sparkle and a warm, happy glow comes into His heart. Your love really pleases Him. But if you or I should forget to tell Him how much we love Him, I know the Lord must feel a little bit sad. It just awes me to think that we can make the heart of almighty God either happy or sad by the way we respond to Him.

I think you and I are pretty good friends by now, so I want to let you in on one of the most spectacular secrets I've ever discovered. Do you know the real reason the Lord Jesus created us? Do you know what is the highest calling He can ever place on our life?

God didn't create us just so He'd have someone to work for Him. He has something even greater planned for us than simply being the faithful servant. You and I were created for the supreme purpose of having an intimate and satisfying love relationship with our Creator, a relationship that gives God just as much enjoyment as it gives us. Wow! What a calling— to be the lover of the King of heaven Himself!

Let's get down to business and try to figure out exactly what it means to have a love relationship with the Lord. I believe that the Lord Jesus wants our Christian life to be a romance with Him—a glorious romance that will grow sweeter and sweeter each day until finally, in heaven at the marriage supper of the Lamb (Revelation 19:1-9), it will be climaxed by our total unity with Him. If someday up in heaven we're going to be made one with Jesus, then we'd better start becoming one with Him down here. We'd better start now to share our life with Him and let Him share His life with us.

You know, that's what true lovers do. They spend hours talking with each other, trying to get to know each other better. When they discover how much they mutually love and admire one another, pretty soon a trust begins to grow between them. They find out they can trust their lover with those deep, personal secrets they never dared to share with anyone else.

That's exactly the way the Lord Jesus wants it to be with us and Himself. Even though He already knows everything about us, He wants us to share our thoughts and feelings with Him as if He were getting to know us for the first time. He wants us to pull off our masks, draw back the curtain that has been hiding the real us, and just be ourselves around Him. The Lord Jesus loves us just the way we are, and we honor Him when we begin to trust His love and reveal to Him those things we've been afraid to let anyone else know about.

But here again, our relationship to Jesus is a two-way street. He wants us to pour out our hearts to Him, but did it ever occur to you that Jesus wants just as much to be able to pour out His heart to you? Since He is a person, He has thoughts and feelings just like we do. He too longs for someone who will love Him enough to be concerned about the things that concern Him, someone who is willing to listen to His secrets and treasure them. It is true that the Lord Jesus wants to minister to our needs with His love. But it is just as true that He wants someone who will minister to Him by being a true friend and lover. I believe you and I want to minister to the Lord Jesus in that way, don't we?

As His lovers, we're going to become vitally involved with Him. Everything we own will belong to Jesus, and everything He owns will belong to us. Now this is really beautiful. It's like signing a blank check and handing it to Jesus, saying, "Okay, Jesus, here's my life. Take anything and do anything You want with me. Please fill in the blank on the check Yourself because,

71

Lord Jesus, I totally belong to You."

But praise the Lord, the transaction doesn't stop there. When we commit ourselves to the Lord Jesus and enter this love relationship, His whole huge heavenly bank account is placed at our disposal. He urges us to take everything from Him that we could possibly need or want because, you see, He totally belongs to us too. Now it looks like we're getting the better end of the bargain. But the wonderful fact of the matter is that what we have to offer the Lord Jesus is so extremely valuable to Him that as far as He is concerned, it's a fair deal.

Giving and receiving love—that's what our relationship to Jesus is all about. Both sides of the coin are important. If we never tell Jesus we love Him, or if we never spend any time alone with Him, our romance with the Lord will fizzle out and die. If we give the Lord a lot of our love but never receive from Him, the relationship will be just as unhealthy. When Jesus whispers in our heart that He loves us, He wants us to believe he's telling us the honest truth.

We'd better not be secretly thinking, "Wow, Jesus, what in the world do You see in me? If You really knew me, it would be impossible for You to love me." No, Jesus wants us to open ourselves up and let His love soak deep down into our hearts. His love is powerful, and if we'll only give it the chance, it will set us free from our prison of fear and guilt. His love will flood our lives with joy, and then we'll finally be free to have the same opinion about ourselves that the Lord Jesus has.

Did you know that when Jesus lived on earth, He had a love relationship with the Father just like the kind of relationship you and I are supposed to have with Him today? It's a beautiful pattern for us to follow, in fact. The Bible doesn't tell us about it in so many words, but it does tell us that Jesus often hiked up into the mountains at night while His disciples were asleep to have a long heart-to-heart talk with His Father.

Jesus was there all alone with His Father for a long time, and I've often wondered what they found to talk about for so many hours. I know I'd give anything for the chance to overhear one of their conversations. Do you feel the same way? Then why don't we follow Jesus as He trudges up that little dirt path that's winding its way through the fig and olive groves? We can crouch down in the billowing grass and we'll be practically hidden; I'm sure they won't mind if we eavesdrop.

The night has drawn its curtain across the world, blotting out the sun. The vivid colors of the daytime have been replaced by poignant etchings of black and silver. And all over the mountainside there is a hushed quietness as if nature is startled by the transformation and has suddenly laid aside her tireless, bustling activity. But the moon—nothing can extinguish the activity of its silver flame. Its slender beams dance everywhere, flickering through the shiny leaves of the olive trees, stopping here to flirt with a frond of grass, flitting over there to camouflage a rock in a mask of brightness. High overhead, myriads of stars vie for attention—but they don't seem like stars at all. They are just little holes cut in the curtain of night, the light of the glory of heaven sparkling through and twinkling down on the head of a lone figure seated on a rock in the middle of the olive grove.

Jesus' sturdy shoulders have fallen into a relaxed slump and His hands are resting contentedly in His lap. From out of the friendly quietness, Someone is talking to Him.

"Son, I'm really proud of You. You worked so hard preaching today. Why, Your sermon lasted at least three hours. I know it's tiring to pour Your heart out to Your audience the way You do."

"My back really ached when I was done."

"I know, but You still kept giving Yourself. So many sick people were healed. I saw the tenderness that flowed out of You when You laid Your hands on their heads, and Son, that really touched My heart.

"But I was even more proud of You when You obeyed Me so beautifully by praying over those loaves and fishes. We're a great team, You and I. Just look at the power that results when our hearts and hands join together in love."

"Yea, I know what You mean, Father. It feels so good to have Your power flowing through Me. When I was standing up there in front of the crowd breaking the bread, My whole being felt exhilarated. And Your presence was so strong around Me, just overshadowing Me. Suddenly I felt completely rested as if I could go on passing out the bread and fish for a million years."

"Well, You did a great job today, and I really, really appreciate it. You couldn't have made Me any happier than You did today."

Jesus blushes slightly as He looks down at His feet. "Thank You, Father," He says modestly.

The little olive trees rustle their leaves into a more comfortable position, and on a distant hill a rooster crows sleepily. Restlessly, Jesus stands up and begins to pace back and forth, side-stepping the crumbling rocks that sit half-hidden in the grass. "You know, Father, it's rough work to live here on earth, trying to teach Your children about You. I get so frustrated sometimes—"

"—I don't blame You."

"Philip really disappointed Me today. I was almost sure that he finally understood that he was supposed to bring all his needs to You so You could meet them. Why, just the other day I had a long talk with him about that very subject."

"Tell me about it, Son. It's good for You to talk it out."

"Yea, I guess You're right. Well, a few days ago I noticed that Philip was really worried about something. On our walk from Bethsaida to Capernaum he kept his head down the whole time, just staring at the dust and pebbles on the road. When the other guys tried to make conversation with him, he didn't pay any attention.

"I questioned him about it later on, and he confided in me that he was upset about his wife and little girls. Things were getting rough financially for them since he was away from his job so much now that he was following Me. He told me that his family hadn't had any bread to eat since the last Sabbath—that was about five days before.

"Well, I tried to explain to Him how loving and sympathetic You are. I told him he should ask You to miraculously give his family bread. Then secretly, later on that night while the other guys were getting ready for bed, I walked to the home of Ezra ben Elia. He's the guy who owns that nice bake shop on King Street. I explained Philip's problem, and then I asked him to have a fresh loaf of bread waiting on the Philip family's doorstep every morning. This was all supposed to be done anonymously, of course. They were never supposed to find out who was sending them the delicious bread. Since Ezra is a real good friend of Mine, he jumped at the chance to do Me a favor. He promised to bring them bread every day for at least a year free of charge. Wasn't that sweet of him?"

The Father smiled back as Jesus looked up into the sky, a happy light glowing from His eyes.

"Philip and his wife were thrilled when the first loaf appeared on their doorstep, and they came running over to tell Me about it. I told them the bread was just a simple answer to prayer and that from now on they should trust You to meet *all* their needs.

"I can still hear Philip saying, 'Okay, Master, You must have told me that same thing sixty-seven times by now. But this time I promise I'll learn . . . You'll never have to tell me to trust God again.'

"So guess what happens this afternoon. That huge crowd needed bread to eat. I thought it would be obvious. It was the same situation, only on a larger scale. I asked Philip what we should do, just to prove that he'd finally learned to trust You. And do you know what he says?"

Jesus sighs as He kicks a loose rock out of His path. A shadow of exasperation flickers across His face; instantly, it is replaced with a quiet sadness. "The poor guy shrugged his shoulders and scratched his scrawny beard. Finally he said to

Me, 'Well, it looks like an impossible mess. Your best bet would be to close the meeting and dismiss everybody. Maybe on the way home they can stop at an inn and buy something to eat.'

"Oh, Father, it seems so hopeless sometimes. Do You think I'll ever be able to make them understand Your love?"

"You just keep trying, Son. Eventually they'll learn—but I'm warning You, it's going to take an awful lot of patience."

Jesus grinned. "Speaking of patience, You should have seen what Bartholomew did the other day. I could have felt insulted if it hadn't been so funny. We were down by the seashore in Capernaum near the fish market. A big group of businessmen and a few Pharisees were standing around listening to Me teach. And since it was about noon and business was beginning to thin out, a few of the fishermen ambled over and stood on the fringe of the crowd.

"Well, Bartholomew was sitting on a half-rotten log right near my feet—he *would* have to sit in front where everybody could see him! For some reason, he can never manage to keep his mind on what I'm saying. And talk about a bored expression! He screws up his face and rolls his eyes as if he's going to die if I don't hurry up and finish.

"I think he was trying to give me a hint or something, but all at once he flung his arms into the air and stretched as hard as he could and then let out an enormous yawn. He opened his mouth so wide I almost fell in. And believe it or not, a fly that was buzzing along just then actually did. Maybe it mistook Bartholomew's mouth for a shady cavern, but anyway it somehow managed to fly down his throat.

"Poor old Bart snorted and grabbed at his neck as if he was going to wring it off. Then he started choking. Somebody yelled, 'Pound him on the back,' and when I did, his rotten log finally caved in and Bart went sprawling across the sand.

"That was too much for everybody. They all laughed their heads off, and of course I burst out laughing Myself. Needless to say, that was the end of My lesson."

The Father chuckled. "If you think it was funny from your point of view, You should have seen it from up here in heaven; even the angels snickered."

Jesus walks over to a sycamore tree and leans His head against its crumpled bark. For a long time He is quiet, studying the shadows in the valley below as if lost in thought. Finally He speaks. "Father, do You know what means an awful lot to Me since I've come to earth to live?"

"What?"

"Having John for My friend. He's such a great guy; I know I really love him—but in a slightly different way than I love the others." Absent-mindedly Jesus tears a leaf off a twig and crushes it in His fingers. "John seems to understand Me in a way that the others don't. I'm sure he knows who I am. Something inside of him is always reaching out to Me. I don't quite know how to explain it, Father—" There is a pause as Jesus hunts in His mind for the right words. "—Well, there's a sort of a deep bond between us—as if words aren't necessary sometimes, because we can still feel a communication running between our hearts. You know, Father, I think I'd be awfully lonely living here if I didn't have John."

"I know. That's why I created John for You—I knew You'd need a best friend while You were living there."

"Thanks. Of course You'll always be My very best Friend, Father. But still, just having You isn't quite enough. I know I really need a human friend too, someone I can see and feel." Again Jesus stops talking. A moonbeam finds its way through the fluttering leaves and plants a silvery glow on His face.

"Do You know what he did this afternoon? Everyone had been fed and we had gathered all the leftovers into big baskets when John stepped over to Me. He slung his arm across My shoulders and, looking Me straight in the eye, he said, 'That was great, Jesus.' Deep in his eyes I could see a well of love for Me that slowly flowed out until it was like a warmth covering

Me. I didn't say anything, but I gave his arm a quick squeeze and then walked away."

"Son," (the Father's voice is hushed and very tender now) "that's just what Your love means to Me. It's wonderful to have You as My Son, but it means everything to Me that You also enjoy being My Friend. You know, I can talk to You better than I can to anyone else on earth."

By now the moon is directly overhead and the shadows have been swallowed into the ground. A contented sigh rustles through the olive trees as they rearrange their pretty leaves to better catch the reflection of the moonbeams. In a mystical softness, peace spreads itself over the mountainside, banishing the fatigue and tensions of the day. Jesus finally finds His way back to the big rock and sits down, cupping His chin in His hands.

"My Son, there's something I want to tell You about. Tomorrow is a special day for Me—I've waited a long time for it to come. You're going to meet one of My precious daughters just before You preach Your Bread of Life sermon, and oh, she's had such a hard life. Her husband died four years ago while she was pregnant, and when the baby came, it was badly deformed. It has a cleft palate, and one of its arms is only a stump. And to make matters worse, the poor little thing has had convulsions every couple of weeks since it was born.

"You're going to heal the baby tomorrow. Its arm will instantly grow out, and the mouth will become normal. Of course it will never suffer from the seizures again. But even more important than healing the baby is the way You're going to minister to the mother. Son, My heart has been anguished over her. For four years her whole world has been black. Every night when she's lying alone on her mat just before she goes to sleep, she sobs as if her heart were broken. And every night I silently weep with her—although she doesn't know it. She thinks she did something to displease Me, and I deserted her, and now I'm raining My judgment down on her. Oh, Son, I love her! I can't stand to see her living this way!"

The grief from the Father's heart is reflected in Jesus' eyes. "But Son, tomorrow I'm finally going to have a chance to step into her life and prove to her My love. You know how much I appreciate You, don't You? Because if it weren't for You, I wouldn't be able to reach her."

"Well, I'm glad to help," Jesus answered quietly. "I'll just relax and concentrate on You, and You be responsible for pouring Your power and wisdom through Me. Who else am I going to meet tomorrow?"

"Peter and Andrew's friend, a man named Matthias. He was their former fishing partner. My Holy Spirit's been working in his heart for a long time; he's been to several of the waterfront meetings. But he's just not willing to follow You if that involves giving up his money.

"So tomorrow when You see him, this is what I want You to do: look at him for a long time without saying a word. Then firmly but quietly, so no one else can hear, say, 'Matthias, I know about those gold coins you've stashed away in the corner of your kitchen near the woodpile. But if your hope is resting in money to make you happy, someday you're going to be severely disappointed. Following Me is the only sure way to a rich life.'

"Those words of wisdom are going to cut into his heart like a fiery sword."

"Will he turn his life over to us then?"

"No, not right away. Not until You've died and come back home to Me. After Peter has been filled with the Spirit like You are now, I'll send him to Matthias' house for a long talk."

There is a long silence again. Jesus gazes up into the velvet midnight sky as if His eyes are searching for His Father's face. When He speaks, it seems like His words hesitate in the chilly air and hang there trembling a moment before they vanish. "Father," He asks, "what will it be like for Me to die?"

The Father doesn't answer right away—at least not out loud.

But onto that lonely mountain there comes a tangible presence that engulfs the trees and the rocks and the wild flowers, bathing them in a security they've never before known. Jesus Himself feels it, for the lines of pain and loneliness on His face soften into the sweetest expression of trust, and His breathing becomes deep and steady. Finally, with the utmost gentleness, the Father whispers, "My precious Son, it's going to be horrible for You to die. You will suffer more than any man who will ever walk the earth. You will have to experience what none of My other children ever will. You see, in order to make room for them in My family, I'm going to have to disown You, Son. I'm going to have to reject You and desert You, leaving You stranded in the hour of Your greatest agony. And Son, even hell itself couldn't be as awful to You as being cut away from Me."

Beads of sweat break out across Jesus' forehead, but again that vibrant presence engulfs Him with its strength, holding Him in its infinite quietness. Finally Jesus looks up. "Father, I'm willing to go through with it." Each word is spoken distinctly, as if it has been wrenched from the depth of His heart.

"But My Son, in that hour on the Cross when Your suffering is at its very worst, when it seems like the sheer weight of grief is going to crush You, annihilate You, I want You to remember that I too am experiencing a blinding agony. My Father-heart will be broken to pieces watching My beloved Son, the darling of My heart, being ripped away from Me and killed."

"But Father, we love them. We're willing to do it because we love them—"

"—And because we want so much for them to be a part of us . . . Son, You need Me right now. Let Me overshadow You and hide You in My love. Just lie down there on the soft grass. Put Your head on that little clump of soil . . . there. Now let Me minister to You. I want to pour My love into Your heart until You feel it just as sweet and just as glorious as You used to up here in heaven."

And so it is that Jesus closes His eyes and falls into a soft, refreshing sleep, all the while being sheltered in His Father's mighty arms.

The Lord Jesus fascinates me. I can't imagine how God could manage to shrink Himself down until He was small enough to squeeze into a human personality and body. How could Jesus be a man like me and yet at the same time be a perfect miniature of God while He was on earth? It almost gets embarrassing sometimes to think that when Jesus lived in Palestine, He did the same trivial things I have to do every day, like washing out His clothes—maybe He washed them in a stream like some of us do here in Timor—or taking the time to sit down and put a bandage on His cut finger or emptying the garbage basket after He and the disciples had a cookout or—or even cutting His toenails! Can you imagine almighty God doing that?

When I was a little boy, I always used to wonder what Jesus looked like when He lived here. I would have loved to have been one of His disciples and to have followed Him around all over the place, watching Him do those wonderful things, and just plain getting to know what He was like. To be honest, I used to get mad at God (or at mamma or papa) for making me be born two thousand years too late.

But now I know that it's not too late to get to know Jesus. The more I find out about Him, the more involved I get in trying to discover even more. His personality really intrigues me. How can anybody be so masculine and strong and yet so gentle all at the same time? How can the same person be both severe and tender? I don't know, but somehow Jesus manages it.

One minute, His eyes blazing with authority, He was ordering the demons to leave that poor man in Gadara. The next minute, He was sitting there talking in the most gentle tone of voice to the guy He had just set free. In just a few minutes Jesus had formed such a deep friendship with him that the poor guy hated to leave Him to go preach the gospel. One day Jesus stooped down to cuddle all the little children in His arms because He wanted to bless them. But just a few days later He was striding through the Temple, slashing at the merchants with a whip, flinging their money boxes, with a mighty crash, to the stone floor.

Wow, Jesus fascinates me! Getting to know Him intimately and having Him become a reality in my daily life has become a thrilling adventure. It's a big enough challenge to keep me busy for the rest of eternity.

5
The Call

Jesus is looking down from heaven today and His heart is very sad. Imagine the King of glory, that precious one who has done so much for us, being heartbroken.

Why is Jesus so sad? Who is it that is giving Him so much pain? If we are honest, I think we have to confess that we are the ones at fault. We are the ones who have hurt Him so badly.

Do you know how we've done it? By ignoring Him. By being too busy to enjoy His love. By carelessly letting sin slip into our lives.

He died an awful death and suffered such horrible agony that it would blow our minds if we got even a little idea of what it was like. He went through all this hell and torment and anguish just so He could set us free from our sins. Just so He could draw us very close to Himself and bring us His abundant life—that fantastic life of heaven lived right here on earth.

But so often we take His love for granted. We get so wrapped up in our job or our housecleaning or going to church meetings or talking to our friends on the phone or spanking our kids or . . . or a bunch of other things that we forget all about Jesus.

We get so horribly busy that we don't have time to sit down for even one hour and just rest in His presence. We're just like those guys in the Bible who left their first love (Revelation 2:4; 3:15-17). Our God is such a good God and He has so much to offer us. But we're often too lazy to take His blessings. We can't be bothered to make the effort to ask Him and seek Him for something new. Maybe we're scared to get jolted out of the nice little rut we've dug ourselves. If we ask Jesus to step into our life and prove to us personally that He's still the same miracle-working God He was in the Bible days, all kinds of things are going to have to change. And we just can't stand to be changed! We're very comfortable the way we are. We sure don't want Jesus or anyone else, for that matter, to disrupt our plans and rock the boat!

I think we even get so used to our problems that it would bug us and make us feel insecure if Jesus ever removed them. "Oh, well, it's been like this for twenty years," we say. "If I could stand it that long, I guess I can stick it out another twenty. Anyway, I've already accepted the fact I'd always have this mess on my hands and now I'm learning to live with it."

But even worse than that, we get used to the sins in our life. We call them "weaknesses" or "personality defects." We tell ourselves, "I can't be perfect, because I'm not God. I'll always have some sin in my life. But that's all right. The Lord loves me and He'll forgive me whenever I make a little 'mistake.' "

But our sins do matter to Jesus. All of them. Even the little ones—like complaining about our job or nagging our husband . . . or staying mad at the kids . . . or not liking our boss . . . or disobeying Him and not visiting Mrs. Smith in the hospital like He told us to . . . (well, I think if we're honest, each of us could fill a pretty long list of our own sins.)

But Jesus is holy, and He just can't stand sin. From the very beginning of the revival the Lord made it perfectly clear to us who was Boss. *He was!* He wouldn't let us get away with any funny business or disobedience. We had to explicitly carry out every single command He gave us. If we didn't—I mean, if we got lazy or didn't think He really meant what He said—He'd have to punish us.

God was trying to teach us that He was our big Daddy and we were His little kids. If we rebelled and tried to go our own way, He'd have to spank us. But, boy, once we said we were sorry, He'd just throw His arms around us, hug us, and kiss us to pieces.

Let me tell you the story. It was the very first day that I joined the teams, 2½ months after the revival started. I remember as I walked up to my team leader and the six other guys on my team. I felt awfully excited—and a little bit curious too. I was wondering what in the world the Lord was going to do for us.

Well, He sure started out with a bang. Just a few hours after we left Soe and started walking toward the village where He had told us to preach, the Lord did a wonderful miracle. I saw it with my own two brown eyes.

You see, the Lord told us to leave Soe early in the evening—around six P.M. And where we live, right on the equator, the sun is usually fast asleep in bed by then. To be honest, we all thought His command was ridiculous and impossible and downright nutty.

How in the world were we ever going to walk up and down those mountains and through those thick forests without a speck of light? To make it even worse, the Lord had told us that we weren't allowed to bring a lantern or even a candle. We were tempted to think that poor Jesus had slipped off His rocker for sure that time.

But thank the Lord, we had enough sense to obey Him that time anyway. And, boy, the Lord sure showed us He knew what He was doing. He's a super-powerful God whose ways and thoughts are far greater than ours are.

Anyway, do you know what He did? He sent a light straight out of heaven and shone it down on the path where we were walking. When we were supposed to turn left, the light pointed toward the left. And it pointed to the right when we were supposed to turn right. I was fascinated that the light could be so smart.

Of course, it's sort of hard to describe what the light looked like. It didn't start from any particular place up in the sky; it wasn't beaming down from a star, for instance. I can only explain it by saying that the light was just *there*. I guess you could say it looked like a moving spotlight or maybe like the landing light of the airplane. (It reminded me of the pillar of fire the Lord used to lead the Israelites in the Old Testament.) But, oh, it was so bright and so beautiful! I had never seen anything like it in my life. It was far brighter than the smoky kerosene lanterns we sometimes used.

I'll never forget the tremendous sense of peace and security I felt that night. God Himself was leading us. I knew we were completely safe in His mighty hands.

Finally around midnight the light came to a dead standstill. We were pretty sleepy by then. So we all curled up in the grass on the side of the path and fell fast asleep.

Around four o'clock the next morning the Lord woke us up and told us to start walking. (Jesus is awfully gentle and loving about the way He wakes somebody up . . . He doesn't grate on your nerves like a screechy rooster or a horrible old alarm clock.) It was really beautiful. Nobody poked each other or even talked to each other, but all of a sudden we all woke up at exactly the same minute. And we felt very refreshed after only four hours of sleep.

So we started walking again. But all at once everything started to go horribly wrong. Things weren't beautiful and smooth like the night before. No, sir! For some awful reason the light wouldn't shine to tell us where to go. We kept on getting stuck and confused. No matter how hard we tried to walk fast, we just weren't getting anywhere. We were so confused! We started to get madder and madder at each other and more and more bewildered and upset and scared until—all at once the disaster happened. I don't know how in the world she managed it, because she was supposed to know the path very well, but suddenly our team leader fell smack, bang, crash into a hole. She twisted her poor foot terribly. And somehow, don't ask me how this could happen, she fell to the ground so hard that she almost died. She just lay there cold as a stone on the side of the path without moving a muscle.

Boy, that scared us silly! Something was really the matter. The Lord just plain wasn't blessing us and guiding us like He had been the night before. Finally it dawned on us that we'd better sit down right there in the dirt path and have a little spur-of-the-moment prayer meeting.

So we did. "O Lord," we all started to pray in our most holy tone of voice, "please show us who is responsible for this big mess we're in. Don't let him get away with it any longer, Lord." Well, I can sure tell you that it didn't take the Lord very long to answer that prayer!

(Excuse me, but I think I'd better interrupt my story to tell you something I forgot to mention before. Before our team left Soe, the Lord had given us very explicit instructions about what we were supposed to do and what was strictly forbidden. It was strictly forbidden, for example, to bring any extra junk along. We weren't allowed to carry any money or shoes or extra changes of clothes or personal belongings or anything. All that was permitted was one day's supply of food and one powder box and mirror for the ladies. We men were pretty disgusted about that last one, but I guess Jesus is more sympathetic than we are.)

Well, anyway, while we were sitting there praying, the Lord gave my friend Joktan a vision. (Do you know who Joktan is? I guess you haven't met him face-to-face yet. But actually he's been peeking out at you from many of the pages in this book. He was there the time Jesus saved that pagan priest out by the big tree in Baob. And he was at the service where that horribly crippled man was healed. When we were little boys, Joktan and I went to school together. And to this day we are still very, very good friends.)

In the vision, Joktan saw everybody walking back to Soe except him. He was the only one left on the team preaching the gospel. Do you know what the interpretation of that vision was? Every single one of us, except my friend Joktan, had done something wrong.

We had brought along a whole bunch of stuff that we weren't supposed to. One girl confessed that she brought a needle and some thread "just in case." Somebody else brought along some money, and one of the guys was carrying a pair of shoes. (Boy, I was really mad at him. I saw him holding them when we were ready to leave Soe and I told him not to bring them. Who did he think he was, anyway?)

My team leader had put a big fancy gold hairpin into her bun, and I guess according to Jesus that was a no-no too. (In Indonesia almost all the ladies wear their hair the same way. They comb it straight back and wind it all into a big knot at the back of their neck. But I found out a secret. Do you want me to let you in on it? If the ladies want to look extra-fancy and they don't have enough hair to make their bun look impressive, they buy a fake one! And somehow they stick it on their head with a whole bunch of pins. Boy, these ladies! They do such crazy things sometimes to try and make themselves look pretty.)

I was so upset! What a bunch of sinners these other team members were! Why, how could they possibly be so disobedient! I was bawling them out and yelling at them for being so stupid, when finally the Lord got it through my thick head that I shouldn't talk. I was a pretty big sinner myself.

Do you know what I had done? I'd brought along a roll of gauze bandages "just in case we have an accident." Well, the Lord sure saw to it that I got what I'd asked for. We had such a bad accident that my team leader was lying there on the ground ready to die.

Pretty soon we all felt so awful about our sins that we started to cry. "O Jesus, please, please forgive us," we sobbed. "We're so sorry we disobeyed You."

I can guess that right now you're thinking, *What in the world is so awful about bringing a few extra things along? Jesus sounds like a real meanie to call that such a big sin.* But you see, the Lord had specifically told us not to bring those things. He was trying to teach us how very important simple obedience is. Just one little sin will disrupt our relationship with Him and cause us a whole lot of problems.

Now actually, those early days of the revival were a special training period the Lord was putting all the team members through. He doesn't give us so many picky instructions today. But He had to teach us right from the very start how tremendously important it is for us to walk close to the Lord and not let even one little sin come between us and Him.

After we had really repented, the Lord healed my team leader so she could start walking again. He told us that we were to walk quickly to the town of Pene and leave all our illegal junk at a certain pastor's house. So off we went.

But do you think I learned my lesson and would never disobey Jesus again? Well, if you said yes, then I'm sorry. You just plain don't know Mel Tari very well yet.

We were walking along having a wonderful, happy time when all at once I spotted a big guava tree up ahead just loaded with ripe, juicy, mouth-watering fruit. Now actually, the Lord hadn't told us that we were allowed to stop and eat yet. In fact, when we started out that day, He had told us that we weren't allowed to pick up any fruit on the way.

Ha, ha, ha, I chuckled to myself, *I bet I can fool Jesus!* So I poked Joktan and said, "Look over there." I was thinking to myself, *If I'm going to get in trouble, at least Joktan is going to get it too.* This whole time I had been simmering mad because Joktan was such a goody-goody that he hadn't gotten a spanking like the rest of us had. "Now, Joktan," I instructed, "we are going to be very obedient servants of Jesus. We're not going to pick up the guavas and eat them because the Lord told us not to. No, we're going to grab the fruit that's hanging on the tree with our teeth. We're going to eat it off the tree like a horse."

And that's just what we did. We stood there chomping away at those poor guavas like a couple of ridiculous dummies. And that's exactly what we were: dummies.

You can guess what was waiting for us up ahead. You see, we had just given the Lord a showcase exhibit of obeying the letter of the law but not the spirit.

As we started to walk again, pretty soon I felt something funny turning round and round in my heart. Yup, everything was starting to go wrong again, just like I had half-suspected it would. Our whole team started to wander round and round in big circles. We walked for hours, but no matter how hard we tried we could never get anywhere. Time and time again we were at the same place we had started out from.

To make matters worse the sun decided he had done a full day's work. Before we knew it, the sky was pitch black. Finally we just couldn't go on any further, because it seemed like every way we turned we were heading for a steep ravine. Boy, by that time I could sure sympathize with those poor Israelites in the wilderness.

So once again we found ourselves sitting in the middle of the path to pray. By that time the funny feeling in my heart had gotten so strong that it only took me a couple of seconds before I blurted out, "Okay, okay, I'm the big sinner this time."

Luckily, Joktan and I weren't the only criminals in the bunch. Another boy had washed out his shirt in the river, when the Lord had told us we were allowed only to take a bath.

Well, we had been crying and confessing our sins and really repenting only a couple of minutes when my dear Jesus decided to do a spectacularly precious thing for us. (My friends, I can sure tell you that my Jesus is by far the sweetest guy I've ever met. Even though He's very strict, it's just absolutely impossible for Him to hold a grudge. The very instant we say we're sorry and really mean it, He so completely forgets about what we've done wrong that, according to Him, we were never bad in the first place. Praise the Lord!)

We were sitting in a big circle on the grass in the pitch-black darkness of the night. Suddenly the windows of heaven were flung open and the glory of God Himself streamed down upon us. We were just bathed in His light. And into our midst stepped the Lord Jesus Himself. Several of the other team members and I saw Him visibly. He was surrounded by so much light that His form wasn't very clear.

But that didn't really matter. We didn't need to see Jesus. We could feel His presence so strongly. So close and so tender and so comforting. Oh, how wonderful it felt! We just luxuriated ourselves in His love. And we let Him wrap the warm, cuddly blanket of His peace and security around us until I was so happy that I knew I was living in heaven at that moment. Like that pretty song says, "Heaven came down and glory filled my soul."

Then Jesus spoke to us. "My precious ones, I know you're tired. I'll lead you to the resting place."

The spotlight moved forward. And once again we had the joy of following it through the forest and up and down the mountains. When it stopped, it was pointing to a big pile of bamboo leaves. Jesus had provided a soft, cozy mattress for us to sleep on that night.

And that's not all He did, either. The next morning we saw a very heavy dew almost like a light rain dripping off the trees and soaking the ground all around us. But there was a large dry area in the shape of a square right where we had been sleeping. During the night the angels must have spread out their beautiful white wings to form a roof over our heads while we slept. No wonder we felt so happy and refreshed when we woke up.

The Lord Jesus really has a talent for blessing us far better than we can dream possible. Could you tell that from the story? Did you see how much it grieves Him when we are not careful and we let some sin come between us? Just one little sin will build up a wall so high and thick that the Lord's love and blessings can't get through.

If we belong to Jesus, then we are obligated to obey Him no matter what He asks, just because we love Him so much. No longer can we be our own boss. Instead, the Lord

Jesus must be our Master in supreme control of every part of our life. He has the right to change anything about us that bothers Him. He has the right to make us obey traffic laws or stop smoking or quit resenting our mother-in-law or start witnessing to our boss, even though we might get ridiculed.

If we are really the Lord's followers, then He has the right to demand that we die to self. Do you know what that means? Well, self is anything that separates us from Jesus and the abundant life. For example, if I am involved in some activity that is keeping me from being as close to Jesus as I possibly could be, then that activity is wrong for me and I must turn my back on it. If I am harboring an attitude that hinders the Lord's peace and joy from flowing into my heart, then I can know that the Lord Jesus is grieved with that attitude and I must "die" to it.

The self that we must die to is that horrible, ugly, black shell that so terribly distorts the beautiful masterpiece that the Lord created us in the first place. Jesus knows we desperately need to get free of that awful shell, so that's why He sometimes brings difficult circumstances into our life. Now if we'll only submit and let the Lord change us—change our attitudes and reactions—when things go wrong, He'll be able to free us from self and restore us to His beautiful image. But if we grumble and complain about our problems, we'll just get in deeper bondage to our ugly self than ever. We must always remember that our problems are the tools God uses to polish us, not demolish us.

Nothing, and I mean absolutely nothing, must be allowed to keep us from being just as close to Jesus as possible. He is to be our only goal. Knowing Him just as well as we possibly can and experiencing just as many of His blessings and gifts as possible is to be our main ambition, yes, the driving force of our life—Jesus must be everything to us.

No longer are we going to be allowed to be a wishy-washy, halfway Christian. We can't turn ninety-five percent of our life over to the Lord but refuse to let Him control that other five percent. Jesus requires that we give Him our all.

Boy, I can sure tell you right now that if you really want to follow Jesus and be a 100 percent disciple, it's going to cost you something. You're going to get jolted out of your comfortable little rut in a hurry. You're going to be thrust out into the battlefield and find yourself face-to-face with the hosts of darkness. You're going to go on an all-out offensive against Satan. The Lord will require you to stand up and fight like His soldier.

The Christian life is a rough, tough challenge. Only those who have an honest commitment to Jesus Christ—not in their mouths or minds but in their hearts—will ever have the guts to stick it out when the going gets rough.

Just look at Jesus. He sure didn't have an easy life while He was on earth. If He hadn't had guts, those Pharisees would have ripped Him to shreds and tossed Him into the Dead Sea. But Jesus had the courage and character to stand up to them. Jesus was a red-blooded, tough Man, the kind of man I admire. I can just see Him standing there by that wildly tossing Sea of Galilee. The storm is whipping His hair around His sunburned face and slapping His coarse robe against His thighs. Like huge pillars His muscular legs are astride, planted firmly in the sand.

Look how His eyes flash fire as He shakes His finger in the Pharisees' faces. "You're a bunch of snakes and hypocrites and fancied-up graveyards, all of you! Don't kid yourselves. God sees your hearts. You're not going to get away with trying to fool Him!" His voice rings out over the water like a trumpet—louder than the crashing of the waves or the screeching of the sea gulls . . . .

Yes, Jesus is our example, and today He is calling us to leave everything and follow Him, to forsake our ninety-five percent way of living and go all out, lock, stock, and barrel, for Him. Are we willing? He is calling us to crown Him the sole Lord and Master of our life.

Today we are forced to make a decision. We can either decide yes or no, but we must decide. Will we go all the way with the Lord Jesus? Will we take up our cross and follow Him?

Maybe you are thinking, *I don't have the courage and determination to stay close to Jesus when the going gets rough. I'll never make it.*

But please listen to me. The Lord doesn't expect you to have the strength in yourself. He'll supply it. In fact, it's important that you know that you are helpless and must depend totally on your God. All He expects you to do is to decide with your will that you want to follow Jesus all the way.

Now you are faced with a tremendous challenge. I am going to ask you to do me a big favor. Please put this book down at the end of this chapter and have a deep heart-to-heart talk with Jesus. Please don't read another page until you have decided who is going to be the boss of your life from now on. Are you willing to obey the Lord no matter how difficult it may be to do what He commands? To repent of any sin that He shows you is grieving Him? Will you let Him drastically change your life to make you into the kind of man or woman He wants you to be?

My friend, I challenge you today.

Dear Lord Jesus, I come to You now and ask You to give my friend the strength to make the right decision. Oh, Jesus, help him to make a total commitment to You. Help him not to hold anything back. Please take away any fear that might by trying to keep him from Your will. Give him the courage to follow in your steps.

(And now will you pray this prayer with me?)

O Lord Jesus, right now I put my whole life into Your precious hands. You can do anything with me that You want to. Please look into my heart and show me anything about me that grieves and displeases You. Oh, Jesus, I'm willing to change and leave that old way of life if You'll only give me the strength. Today, Lord, is the beginning of my deep and new commitment to You.

6
Let the Wind Blow

Did you decide to go all-out for Jesus just now? Then I know He is really proud of you! You have just proven to Him how much you love Him and how very much He means to you. I tell you, Jesus doesn't take your commitment to Him for granted. No, He really appreciates your love.

But like I said before, you don't have to try to live up to your commitment on your own. In fact, you're not supposed to. Somebody has been given the special task of doing the whole job for you.

May I please introduce Him to you? My friend, I would like you to meet *the Holy Spirit.*

"Holy Spirit, this is my friend ———. (I'm sorry, I don't know your name, but, praise the Lord, we can be friends anyway.) Holy Spirit, my friend is a real nice guy who wants You to help him become more like Jesus. There might still be a couple of rough spots on his life that need some attention. But that's all right; we know it won't be a bit hard for You to smooth them out."

Wow! I can tell you from experience that the Holy Spirit has a real talent for making life exciting. He's going to transform you so that you can finally experience His genuine, undiluted, abundant life. Believe me, there can be no greater happiness on earth than when we live our lives the way God planned for us to live it. When we pattern our lives after the Lord Jesus Christ, we're going to feel a satisfaction we never dreamed possible.

I can't read your mind right now, so I don't know what you're thinking. But please don't feel for one minute that God might leave you out. His wonderful life is for *you* just as much as it is for me or anyone else in this world. I don't care how full of sin you are; I don't care if you have a history of nothing but failures and mistakes; the Lord can transform *you* to be just as sweet and holy as Jesus is. Maybe you are overwhelmed by problems; your life is full of darkness at this moment. But you do not need to be discouraged, because the Lord Jesus wants to step into your situation and fix up the whole mess. He can transform your life to be a carbon copy of His own life, victorious and radiant.

I know a little song that says exactly what I'm trying to tell you. It goes like this: "The Savior can solve every problem / The tangles of life He'll undo / There is nothing too hard for Jesus / There is nothing that He cannot do."

Boy, that's really true. There's nothing too hard for Jesus. He gets all excited about stepping into an impossibly horrible situation and transforming it into something unbelievably wonderful. In fact, I think you could say that's the Lord's favorite hobby.

I just thought of a nice illustration to show you what I mean. You already know that the Lord has changed water to wine for us many times since the revival started. But did you ever think of the spiritual significance behind that miracle? He's taking some drab, uninteresting water—of course, water is awfully nice too, but for the sake of the story, just think about how boring it is—He takes a bucket of unexciting water and transforms it into the most delightful wine.

In this particular incident though, the Lord did something even more impressive. He didn't start out with ordinary water. No, He decided He was going to make His real nice brand of wine out of some stinky, putrid stuff even the cows didn't like to drink.

When the Lord told a lady in our church that she was supposed to pray over that stuff, she was shocked. She'd had lots of experience praying to Him to change water to wine. In fact, He'd used her that way more than twenty times.

Well, this particular time (it was in July of 1973) He told her she was supposed to fast and pray for three days. That part was fine. The Lord usually instructed her to do that before she went to fetch the water.

Then He told her to do something new. She was supposed to go to the pastor of my church and ask him for some money to buy a big plastic bucket. Then she was told to go over to his house and clean a certain bedroom that would be used as a prayer room. The room wasn't terribly dirty in the first place, but out of love to Jesus she wanted it to look as nice as possible. So with a little grass broom she swept the floor and then put some fresh flowers she had picked from the pastor's garden in a vase. Finally, when everything else looked just right, she put the prettiest sheets she could find on the bed. (In Timor the ladies love to embroider and crochet with cotton thread. So the sheets she found were probably quite fancy with a whole bunch of embroidered squiggles and flowers and some other stuff that I'm not quite sure what to call them.)

Anyway, when she was finished doing all of that, the Lord told her to go to the pool of water near the pandanus tree, fill her new bucket with the water, and bring it back to the special room to pray over it.

(Do you know what a pandanus tree is? It's a crazy-looking tropical tree that grows in shallow water. All its roots stick way up out of the ground so that the poor tree is balanced high up in the air. It gives you the feeling that it's tottering around on tiptoe about to fall over any minute.)

When the little lady (by the way, her name is Sister Johanis) got to the pandanus tree, she was shocked. Why, that water was dirty and stagnant. There were a bunch of rotten logs and dead weeds floating around in it. And to be plain honest with you that water *stunk!*

(Now that may be a pretty good picture of our own lives sometimes—a rotten, unhappy mess.)

"Oh, Lord, I'm afraid You've made a horrible mistake. You don't know what You're doing!" She was so upset that she couldn't help but give Jesus a piece of her mind. "I'm sure You don't want to use this junk. Why don't You tell me to get that nice fresh water over there in the spring?"

Then Jesus had to bawl Sister Johanis out a little bit. Of course He knew what He was doing! He was the almighty, wise God, wasn't He?

"Listen to Me, daughter," He spoke in her heart. "When I tell you to do something, I expect you to obey Me. Don't ask so many questions. Don't try to be so smart that you end up like a fool. After all, I'm the Boss around here, and I have all power to do anything I want."

(And that's the way it always is. Before the Lord can do a miracle for us, before He can transform our "mess" into a beautiful new life, we have to let Him be the Boss. We won't see a miracle until we've set Him free, by our obedience and willing heart, to work in us.)

Sure enough, that problem wasn't too hard for Jesus to solve. It was no trouble at all for Him to change that icky water into sweet-smelling, purplish-red wine. After praying over the covered bucket in the special bedroom for a few days, the Lord told Sister Johanis to lift the lid. And there it was. Just as delicious as you could ever hope for wine to be. About eight hundred people had the privilege of sipping some of it when Pastor Daniel served it at a Communion service in our big church.

Now if Jesus cared enough about the miserable water to turn it into something so nice, you can be sure He cares far more about you. You can also be sure the Holy Spirit is capable of fixing you up just right.

If you give Him the chance, I guarantee that the Holy Spirit is going to do an unexplainable miracle in your life. He is a real, dynamic force and He will accomplish what you never thought was possible. You won't have to fake it and just pretend you've been changed, and you won't have to muster up the miracle by yourself. All you have to do is let the winds of His power blow through your life, and all of a sudden you'll find out He's made you different. He had done what you've never been able to do yourself, no matter how hard you've tried.

I used to have a terrible problem with lying. Ever since I was a little boy, I'd tell a fib whenever I needed to get out of a jam. I used to steal the eggs from mamma's pet hens, for instance, and run off to the forest where nobody could see me. I'd build a little fire out of some dead branches and cook my eggs in a tin can, and wow! nothing tasted better to me than those boiled eggs. When I'd finally sneak back home, mamma would be waiting for me.

"Mel, did you take my eggs?" she'd ask. "I can't imagine where my hens laid them today."

"No, mamma," (I acted as innocent as an angel), "I didn't take them." And then I'd run off to play.

When I got bigger, I had to lie to my schoolteachers to try to stay out of trouble. I remember a physics teacher in ninth grade. None of us liked him because he was so strict and mean, so we were always trying to think up tricks to make him mad. I was going to the big high school in Kupang at the time, which sat right at the bottom of a very steep cliff. In the rainy season the water would come swooshing down that hill and would have flooded our classroom if we hadn't kept the door to the outside tightly shut and built a little dam of rocks in front of it.

One day all of us kids who especially disliked that teacher got together to brainstorm, and I must confess that I was one of the ringleaders. We decided to flood our classroom in order to turn our teacher into a soggy, dirty mess. So before our physics teacher came in, we real quick opened the outside door and tore down the dam. The filthy, muddy water gushed into the room until it was at least eighteen inches deep. Of course, none of us wanted to get wet, so we scrambled up onto our desk tops and stuck our feet in the air.

When our poor teacher opened the other door that led to the hall to walk into our classroom, all that icky water rushed out to greet him. It almost knocked him off his feet. That day he happened to be wearing a spotlessly white shirt and a spotlessly white pair of pants. By the time our prank was over he had brown splotches all over his clothes and his pants were stained up to the knees as if he'd been splashing around in a mud puddle.

Needless to say, our trick worked; our teacher got good and mad, and I was the first one he yelled at.

"Mel, you horrible boy! I bet you're behind this whole thing!"

"No, I'm not," I snapped back, "I didn't have a thing to do with this." Of course, that was an out-and-out lie, but my friends were too loyal to squeal on me. To be honest, I didn't feel guilty about lying, because I was so glad it had saved me from a paddling.

But by the time I was eighteen or nineteen, just before I asked Jesus to come into my heart, my lying started to bother me. I read in my Bible that lying was an abomination to God. I wasn't quite sure what an abomination was, but I knew it was pretty bad. That scared me, because I was addicted to lying; I just couldn't quit.

By then I was out of school, so every day I'd walk with my sister to the office where she worked as a secretary. Life is very easygoing in Timor and nobody gets up-tight about trying to work hard. We usually spent most of the day sitting around telling stories with lots of our friends. My stories were really humdingers; they were always the best, but that was because I'd stretch the truth or invent things to make the story more exciting. When I was bragging about something I'd done, I'd tack on a few juicy (fake) details so that I could outdo the other guy. I'd even boast about something stupendous I'd done—which I actually hadn't done at all. One of my other friends had done it.

In Indonesia we call this "selling the medicine." In the big cities we have some people who sit by the side of the road trying to sell their homemade medicine. They yell out a long list of twenty different diseases their medicine is supposed to cure, when actually all it will do is fix up a sore throat. Well, I guess my brand of "medicine" was popular, because it really sold well; all my friends were fascinated by my stories. They thought I was tremendous.

But I didn't. I was really mad at myself. Every day while walking to the office I would say to myself over and over, "Mel, don't lie; Mel, don't lie; Mel, don't lie." But it never worked, because five minutes after I got there I'd forget and start telling another false story.

I just couldn't remember not to lie. One day I got a smart idea. I took a pen and wrote on my arm, "Mel, don't lie," except in Indonesian it looked like this: MEL, DJANGAN BERDUSTA.

On the way to the office, each time my arm would swing it would remind me what I wasn't supposed to do. I was pretty proud of myself, because I thought I'd finally get through a whole day without lying. But I couldn't stare at my arm forever, and once while I had it behind my back, before I knew it I was in the middle of another lie.

I was horribly discouraged. "Mel, it doesn't do any good to write 'Don't lie' on your arm," I told myself. "You need to write it on your heart somehow." But I surely didn't know how to do that. I finally decided I wasn't religious enough, so that night I tried to stay up all night to pray. I knelt down by the side of my bed, but soon I started to get sleepy . . . the next thing I knew it was morning and I found myself in a crumpled heap on the floor.

It was no use. I was a hopeless case. No matter how hard I tried, I just couldn't quit lying.

But one day I met the Lord Jesus. I invited His Holy Spirit to step into my life, and praise the Lord, I wasn't a hopeless case to the Holy Spirit. I don't know how in the world He ever managed it, but somehow He had enough power and wisdom to help me quit lying. From then on, when I'd go to the office and a spectacular, untrue story would pop into my head, the Holy Spirit was right there to whisper in my heart, "Mel, don't say it!"

Things went a lot more smoothly once the Holy Spirit was there to remind me. Gradually I quit struggling and started to relax. The less I worried about lying the more He helped me not to do it. It wasn't long before I realized that the Holy Spirit had set me completely free from a problem that had bugged me as long as I could remember.

Now I've already introduced you to the Holy Spirit—the wonderful One who is in charge of transforming your life. But before He can get to work and really start fixing you up, you are going to have to complete a very important transaction. You are going to have to sign your life away. You won't belong to yourself any longer; every bit of you will belong to Him. Actually, this transaction has another fancy spiritual name. If you want to, you could call it "being filled with the Spirit."

When you became a Christian, the Holy Spirit came into your life and began to dwell inside of you (whether you knew it or not). But nine chances out of ten, you've treated Him more like a guest than like the Master of the house. You've only invited Him into your living room (into your spiritual activities, like going to church or having your devotions in the morning).

Being filled with the Spirit isn't a matter of you getting more of Him. The real question is, does He have all of you? Have you placed every bit of yourself into His care and keeping? Is every part of your life under His control?

The Holy Spirit doesn't want to live only in the spiritual section of your life. The other parts are every bit as important

102

to Him—your business or your housework, your relationship with your friends, what you do on your day off, and how you discipline your kids. The Holy Spirit wants to get vitally involved in all these activities. He wants to determine which TV programs you watch just as much as He wants to decide which person you should witness to. He wants to help you have fun at the parties you go to just like He wants to help you enjoy your daily Bible reading. He is as concerned about healing you of your Monday morning depression as He is about making sure there is no sin in your life. Both the little and the big things are equally important to Him.

The Holy Spirit is asking you to fling open all the doors of your heart and give Him a sweeping invitation. "Come on in, Holy Spirit, you are welcome in every room of my house. Search them and examine them in every place—in all the drawers and closets, under the beds, behind the sofas. Look everywhere.

"Then throw away anything You don't like and clean up all those grimy places I've been trying to hide. You're the Boss now, so completely remodel me if You want to. I'll just trust that You have awfully good taste and know what is best."

After the Holy Spirit has cleaned you up and redecorated you and filled your house with the sweet perfume of His love and power, you will discover that He has transformed you into a beautiful palace, fit for the King of Kings Himself. You'll begin to sense His presence in your life. Yes, Jesus will become more and more real to you.

I believe this is the Holy Spirit's desire and goal: to transform us to be like Jesus. Nothing makes Him happier than to watch us start to sparkle and shine just the way our beautiful Master does. Nothing thrills Him more than seeing the purity, the sweetness, and the strength of our Lord stamped across our personality.

But the Holy Spirit knows a lovely secret. He knows we'll never be able to do one single little thing to change ourselves. *He* has to do the whole job. He is the only One who is smart enough to figure out what needs to be done and then strong enough to do it.

In other words, He is not only the Captain of our ship (to decide where we're going), but He's also the mighty Wind that fills the sails of the ship and sends it skimming across the water.

I wish we could talk a little bit more about *exactly how* the Holy Spirit is going to transform our life once we've given Him complete control. To me this is a fascinating subject.

Well, I believe that the Holy Spirit is very smart. He's going to start fixing us up in the place where we need it the worst. He's going to begin His repair job on the most personal and most important area of our life. This is the area the Bible calls our *heart*. After we've been filled with the Spirit, we'd better get ready for Him to go to work remodeling our heart.

"But what's my heart?" you ask. Well, let me try to help you figure it out. Everybody's heart is in a different place. The thing that is more important to you may not concern me a bit. So in order to figure out what are your biggest concerns, please answer these questions—and please be as honest as possible. (You probably won't be able to zip through these questions, because they might take quite a bit of thought.)

1. What is your biggest goal or ambition?
2. What is your deepest need?
3. What do you desire more than anything else in this world?
4. If you really think hard, what would give you the greatest satisfaction and happiness in this life?

Do you have a rough idea of where your heart is now? Well, in case you're still a little bit confused, let me give you a few examples of where it might be. Maybe your deepest need is for security. You want to have a nice enjoyable life where everything is pretty much the way you want it to be. You want to be free from things that might worry or disappoint you, and you certainly don't want to suffer because you can't have the things you really want. Your need is for peace and contentment.

Maybe you're starving for love. You long to feel that someone needs you and wants you and thinks you're important. Your heart is aching with loneliness, but so far it seems like nobody is interested in the real you.

It's possible that money means more to you than anything else. Your goal is to be able to buy anything you want. You feel like you will be the happiest if you can have a pretty house, a few nice cars, beautiful clothes, and enough money in the bank.

I know some people whose main ambition in life is to make themselves good enough. They are perfectionists and are always trying to measure up to some standard. But usually no matter how hard they try, they never reach a point of satisfaction where they feel like they have finally made it.

Now maybe you're not like that at all. Maybe you don't care at all about struggling to be good. All you really care about is a special person, like a boyfriend or girlfriend, or your family. Your real happiness comes from your relationship to other people. They are really the most precious part of your life.

Now if you're like me (the way I was before the Holy Spirit grabbed hold of me) then your biggest satisfaction will come from being your own boss. You'll just love to make your own decisions, and it will make you feel really powerful to just go ahead and do whatever you want, no matter what.

Oh, there is one more thing I almost left out. I know many nice people whose lives are centered on being nice Christians. They just love going to meetings—especially nice charismatic ones. They get such a wonderful blessing from the fellowship. Why, they could hardly live without their Christian friends. They're just so thankful that they have been baptized into the Holy Spirit so they could enter this exciting new life.

Some other guys go even a step farther. The most important thing in their life is serving the Lord. They are passionately on fire for Him. They see such a tremendous work to be done and so little time to do it. Their deepest desire, their constant prayer, is to be used of God.

This survey doesn't cover everything, of course. The center of your life may be entirely different than the areas just mentioned, but I hope you've picked up a clue about what is most important to you.

Now, how does knowing where our heart is apply to being filled with the Holy Spirit?

Please read this verse with me:

"You shall love the Lord your God
with all your *heart*,
and with all your *soul*,
and with all your *mind*,
and with all your *strength*" (Mark 12:30).

Here's our answer. When we turn our life over to the Holy Spirit so that He can fill us, He's going to change us until we really do love the Lord with every single part of our whole being.

"You shall love the Lord your God with *all your heart.*" *Wow!* That's a pretty big command! If I'm going to love Jesus with all my heart, then of course I must let Him be my *Master.* I can't make my own decisions anymore. For the rest of my life I will be obligated to give Him instant and complete obedience, no matter what He asks me to do.

Jesus is also going to be my *Source.* I'll have to stop trying to get my security or love from other people. I'll have to stop looking to money or nice circumstances to make me happy. I'll quit struggling so hard to be good and do everything right.

If the Lord Jesus is going to be my Source, then I must look to Him and Him only to meet my needs. All of my security must come from *Him.* Instead of trusting in circumstances, I'll have to trust my Savior to provide for me and keep me happy.

If Jesus is really my Source, then my great longings for love will be satisfied. His opinion of me will be all that matters. I'll let His smile of approval and understanding soak down into my heart. My whole life will be open to His love.

Instead of expecting money or other people to give me a happy life, I'll spend hours alone with Jesus, just getting to know Him and cultivating His friendship. My relationship with Jesus will completely satisfy me so that I won't need to depend on anything else.

Praise the Lord, I'll also be able to quit my struggle to be good. Jesus is my righteousness, and He fulfilled the Law for me so that I don't have to worry about it. All I have to do is to let Him live through me. He'll do all the work while I just relax and enjoy Him.

If I really love the Lord Jesus with all my heart, then He's going to be even more to me than my Master and my Source. He's also going to be my *First Love.* I'll care more about my relationship to Him than anything else. Spending time with Him will be my hobby. In fact, I'll enjoy being with Him more than I could ever enjoy being with my family or anyone else I love.

Jesus will be the dearest person on earth to me. He won't seem like a vague spiritual being far away in heaven anymore, but I'll realize that He has feelings, thoughts, desires, and plans just like I do. I'll be fascinated by His personality and I'll want to get to know Him just as well as possible. In fact, getting to know Jesus will be the goal of my life.

But do you know what else? My life will stop being centered on all the nice Christian activities and meetings I love to attend and will start to be centered on *Jesus Himself.* All the fellowship and spiritual blessings in the world won't be worth half as much as the joy of knowing Jesus in a personal, intimate way. I'll stop seeking only the nice blessings and instead seek the One who wants to bless me.

Now this might surprise you, but I'm even going to quit letting the goal of serving the Lord dominate my life. Even my spiritual works for the Lord are not enough. No, if Jesus is going to be my First Love, then He demands that I be occupied mainly with Himself. He doesn't want me to work real hard for Him half as much as He wants me to simply abide in Him. Abiding in Jesus—that means to feast on His love; to enjoy sweet fellowship with Him, to minister to His heart by spending time with Him.

My friend, if you're really abiding in Jesus, you don't have to worry about whether He'll use you to help Him or not. He *will!* It will be a very natural by-product of your relationship. You won't even have to ask Him to use you. It will automatically happen.

But that's not your business. You're not supposed to think or worry about that. Jesus will take care of it in His own perfect way. All you are supposed to concentrate on is getting close to Jesus yourself.

There is nothing that we can do to honor and please the Lord Jesus more than by giving Him our whole heart. When we let Him control and possess the deepest part of us—well, I'm sure we fill His heart with joy.

Do you remember the story of Mary with her alabaster box of ointment? She gave Jesus the most precious thing she had, and just how very much her love meant to Him.

Jesus sank wearily onto the red and gold striped couch, kicking off His dusty sandals and tugging His fingers through His windblown hair. It had been a rough day and He was really exhausted. Why, they must have walked at least fifteen miles since morning. That road leading from the wilderness near Ephraim was no fun. It was actually no more than a rocky trail, twisting its way around jagged boulders, with a sharp drop-off on one side and sullen caves that lurked with thieves on the other. They had to be on the lookout every minute.

But to make matters worse, all day Jesus had been gripped by a heaviness and a foreboding He just couldn't shake off. He was on His way to Jerusalem now, and He knew what a horrible ordeal was waiting for Him. Ever since Lazarus' resurrection the pressure had been mounting steadily inside. Sometimes it almost seemed more than He could bear.

A servant-boy, supporting a bronze washing basin on his hip, tapped Him gently on the shoulder. "Rabbi, would you like me to wash your feet?"

"Ah, yes!" Jesus' tired face lighted up with a smile. "That will feel so good!" And sure enough, as the cool water trickled over His dusty, sweaty feet, Jesus began to relax.

The room was alive with happy chatter as the guests called noisy greetings to their friends just entering the carved oak doors of the banquet room. Servants strode back and forth between the kitchen and the tables, their bare feet slapping on the cold gray of the pavement. Some balanced huge silver trays of food on their shoulders, while others lit the little oil lamps perched on shelves in the stone walls. Pretty soon the room was dancing with golden light and merrily flittering shadows.

Most of the guests were already reclining on the colorful couches circling the low tables, tossing jokes back and forth to pass the time. Everyone was hungry. With the smell of the cracklings of roast lamb and of freshly baked cornbread drifting into the farthest corners of the room, how could anyone's stomach help but grumble in impatience?

"Hey, Lazarus," John said, reaching around Simon Zealotes to poke his host in the ribs, "when are we going to eat? I'm starved."

"I don't know; you'd better ask the boss. She runs the show around here." Lazarus shot a dirty look in Martha's direction, who had just pushed her way through the swinging door from the kitchen. Martha reached out to slap him and *crash!* The platter of roast lamb she'd been holding went splattering on the floor. "Wow, Martha, you're horribly clumsy," Peter yelled. "You remind me of a donkey in a pottery shop."

"Oh, shut up, you guys! Quit teasing me or you're not going to get any supper at all!"

Everybody laughed. That was sure an idle threat. Why,

Martha's pride and joy was her enormous feasts, and tonight it looked like she'd outdone herself.

In no time at all the tables were loaded with steaming bowls of the most delicious food imaginable. The minute the blessing was over, Peter stuffed three black olives into his mouth and mumbled to Judas to pass the boiled fish. Matthew took a huge serving of the roast lamb while while Jesus helped Himself to a bowl of lentil soup.

"How do you like it, Master?" Martha's sun-browned face was wrinkled with an anxious frown as she stood over Him watching Him dip his bread into the soup.

"Oh, Martha, it's terribly good. I never tasted anything like it. You're a good cook." Jesus looked up at her, tenderness softening the lines on His face. How hard she always worked. Why, she must have spent several days getting all this food ready.

Martha blushed, absent-mindedly shoving a lock of gray hair back under her head covering. "Oh, well, Master, it's nothing really. I got the recipe from David ben Ezra's wife down the street. I was hoping you'd like it."

"Well, I really do. Sit down, Martha. It seems like I hardly ever get a chance to talk to you—"

"Oh, I'm sorry, Jesus, but I just don't have time. I have to run back to the kitchen to make sure the servants aren't goofing things up out there. I'm sorry, Master, I'd like to talk to You too. Maybe sometime later, because right now I'm just too busy."

And before Jesus knew what was happening, she was scurrying out the door, her gray robe swishing after her. He leaned His elbow on the low, linen-covered table and smiled to Himself. *Martha, Martha, still the same old girl. Always so terribly busy trying to make things nice for Me. Oh well, I guess that's the only way she knows to show Me that she loves Me.*

"Say, Master!" A heavyset man by the name of Simeon clapped his hands to get Jesus' attention. "That was sure a super-duper miracle you did the other day. Why, I was never so shocked in my whole life as when I saw Lazarus come walking out of the tomb. I thought I was going to faint dead away."

Lazarus grinned broadly. "If you think you were surprised, what about me!" He chuckled to himself and then said, "Jesus, please pass me some of that boiled fish."

"Sure. Well, how does it feel to be alive?"

"Just great!" He piled a little more fish into his bowl. "And Master, it sure is good to have You here with us. Every time I see you it seems like I feel the thrill of Your power flowing through me all over again. Thanks again for the miracle; I never knew life could be so wonderful."

Jesus grinned back at him, and then He sighed deeply. Yes, it felt good to be back in Bethany. It was nice to have friends who loved Him. They always did their very best, whenever He was in their home, to make Him as comfortable as possible. Here was one place where Jesus felt like He could relax from the tensions of His public ministry. *And you know,* Jesus thought wistfully to Himself, *while I'm here I don't feel quite so homesick for my Father and my real home in heaven.* Jesus stared absent-mindedly at His food, unconscious of the jokes and laughter of the others.

Heaven. It wouldn't be too long now before he'd finally be there. Pretty soon He'd be in His Father's arms again. But oh, what suffering He'd have to go through first! What terrible agony was waiting just ahead of Him. Once again the dark thoughts rose to the surface in His mind. In just a few days He would be tortured beyond endurance, tormented until He experienced hell itself.

Even as He thought about it, the sweat broke out on His forehead. Like a sinister shadow the Cross loomed up in His mind—that horrifying, black, cruel Cross. *Oh, God! Help me to do it!* He pled in His heart. *You know I'm willing.* But already the darkness of His hour—the hour He'd been preparing for since the day He was born—was beginning to close in around Him. He could feel the pressure of it building up steadily until sometimes He could hardly breathe.

Jesus lay there on His couch, silent and grim, His face downward, His hands working nervously. The noise of the party swirled around Him, but Jesus was lost in His own world.

"Master." So softly, so gently a form knelt beside Him. Tenderly, a cool hand smoothed His aching forehead. It was Mary.

"Oh, Master!" she whispered again, her face lined with pain and grief. "How can you bear it!" A sob caught in her throat, and before she knew it she was crying as if her heart were broken.

"Oh, Jesus, my precious Master! I love you!" she sobbed. "Oh, I'd gladly go with You if only I could."

She knelt there on the cold stone pavement, her face buried in the crook of her arm, her tears drenching the sleeve of her dark blue robe. Mary's heart *was* broken. Her Master was going to be killed—crucified, He had said. On His last visit He had tried to describe to her the cruelty of that death. But He had also told her that He was dying because He loved her. He was going to suffer that terrifying ordeal just so that He could someday take her to heaven with Him to live with their heavenly Father.

Mary could hardly bear it. Ever since Jesus had explained this to her, she had spent most of her time alone in her room, thinking and weeping. So soon He would be gone, and there was so little she could do.

Mary fought to control her sobs. "Master!" Her voice was urgent now. "I know Your—Your hour has almost come. I—I want to do something to show I love You. Jesus, please, I want to give You this."

From the folds of her robe she drew a small, white stone object. Jesus gasped. The alabaster box!

Long ago Mary had shown it to Him. It was her dowry present of incomparable value, from Jotham ben Isaac, the man to whom she had been betrothed, who had died suddenly right before their wedding.

There it lay, gleaming in her hand like the rare jewel that it

112

was. Its soft curves shimmered in the lamplight, and shadows flickered and danced across the intricate carvings of its lid until the box seemed to vibrate with life and beauty.

Suddenly, Mary gave the box a sharp, hard crack. The exquisite alabaster broke in half, and out of its heart poured the sweetest, most delightful fragrance Jesus had ever smelled on earth. Only the perfumes nurtured in the gardens of heaven could be compared with this.

Ever so carefully Mary let the spikenard trickle over His head and soak into His hair. Little drops of ointment found their way to His beard and dripped down onto His robe. With the remainder Mary anointed her precious Master's feet. She bathed them in the ointment, and she kissed them. She cradled them in her hands and gently wiped them dry with her cascade of thick, dark hair. Her Jesus. This was all she could do to show Him she loved Him.

Like the current of a mighty river, a deep joy surged into Jesus' being. It radiated from His face as He looked up into Mary's tear-stained eyes and smiled His gratefulness. Never before had anyone given Him the ultimate honor of crowning Him the King of their love. Other people loved Him, He knew that. Martha and Lazarus loved Him, but in their own way, of course.

But only Mary knew the secret way to win His heart. She was the only one who understood Him. Mary could feel His pain, she could sense His suffering, and someday she would share His glory!

Yes, He was ready. Now He was strong to fight and conquer all the horror and blackness that lay ahead of Him. He knew His love would triumph. He would win the victory for His beloved one so that throughout all the ages of eternity they could be one in a love that would never die.

To be one with us in a beautiful love. That's our Jesus' heart's desire. And oh, how He longs for someone who will love Him completely, someone who will entrust Him with every speck of their being and will share their whole life with Him.

You and I want to love Jesus like Mary did, don't we? We want to thrill and satisfy His heart. But how can we do it? We've already talked about giving Him the deepest, most important part of our life—our heart. But I believe we should give Him the ordinary, everyday, insignificant parts of our life that normally we wouldn't dream of sharing with Him as well.

So let Jesus keep you company as you wash the dishes; discuss your day with Him as you ride home from work at night. Tell Him when you have a stomach ache or when you're just plain in a bad mood. Even when you don't feel like praying, be honest and tell Jesus that too. It's wonderful to discover how understanding He is.

Once you start inviting Him into this side of your life, He's going to become an awfully good Friend in a hurry. You're going to find out that you *never* have to feel embarrassed around Him. Why? Well, when the Lord Jesus says He loves you, He means He loves you no matter what. Nothing you do or say will ever make Him love you any less.

And He just plain likes you, too. He wants to have a lot of fun with you, but how's He ever going to do it if the only time you ever talk to Him is when you're in a spiritual mood? He must get bored stiff sitting all alone in your living room when all the action's going on in the back of the house.

Life is going to be exciting when you live every day of it, every minute of it, hand in hand with Jesus. Honesty puts the spice into your Christian life; it's what makes your relationship to Jesus practical. When you start to tell Jesus about everything that happens to you, then you're going to feel His love and presence all day long.

Let me show you how it works. (Remember, the secret is to never get embarrassed and try to hide anything from the Lord.)

When your kids drive you crazy, say, "Lord! Billy and Tommy are such horrible brats! I can't stand them! How in the world did I ever manage to get such ornery kids!" (It helps to

114

take your tensions out on Jesus, because then you don't have to take them out on Billy and Tommy.)

Or when your feelings get hurt, say, "Lord, why does my wife always have to be so crabby? Can't she see that I'm tired when I get home from work? I wish she'd be a little bit considerate for a change." (Until you tell Jesus how you feel, His comfort can't get through to you.)

"Oh, Jesus," you might end up saying sometime, "I did something bad a few minutes ago. I'm kind of ashamed to tell You, but I got mad at my neighbor because she threw my son's ball in her garbage when he accidently kicked it over her fence. I called her a 'nasty witch,' stomped into my house, and slammed the door. I'm really sorry." Pretty soon you'll feel a deep peace welling up inside. You'll know you are completely forgiven; Jesus' love will give you the strength to go over and apologize.

Or you might have a really awful day when everything goes wrong. It's drizzling miserably as you leave for the office, and on the way you get a flat tire. Halfway through the morning your boss bawls you out because you're late in handing in a report, and just half an hour later your wife calls you on the phone to announce that your baby had to be rushed to the hospital because he swallowed six aspirins. As each thing happens, make sure that you pour out your frustration on Jesus. If you get mad, tell Him! And if you start to get depressed, make sure you share your feelings with Jesus. When you walk through your day with Him, you won't collapse in a frazzled heap at the end of it.

But don't only share the bad moments with Jesus. Tell Him about the nice ones too. For instance, when you're awed by the beauty of His creation, say something like, "Lord, this rose is a masterpiece! It seems like its petals are made from crimson velvet, and it smells just the way heaven must smell. You must have transplanted it from Your own garden just for me."

When your friend lovingly squeezes your hand as you leave church on Sunday morning and a warm glow spreads across your heart, tell Jesus about it. When you realize that your friend's love is just a little picture of the Lord's love for you, Jesus will seem extra close and precious.

"Jesus, this afternoon I baked a cake," you might tell Him when you're feeling sort of proud of yourself. "I don't mean to brag or anything, but it tasted stupendously delicious. It makes me feel so creative when something I do turns out right."

Do you get the idea? Talk to Jesus about everything that happened. Let me say it again. Tell Jesus about *everything!*

This will give Him a chance to step into your situation and prove how much He loves you. All day long you'll feel His grace working to help you. When you share your whole life with Jesus, then He can share His love and power with you. The more of these insignificant incidents you share with Jesus, the more real His presence will become to you. Pretty soon you'll feel Him right beside you every place you go; you'll enjoy His companionship in everything that you do. This is the great joy of being a Christian, because "in Thy presence is fulness of joy; in Thy right hand there are pleasures forever" (Psalm 16:11).

In Timor we know by experience that nothing is too insignificant for Jesus. We have learned to tell Jesus about the small things that bother us, and usually before we know it, He's already solved our problem.

My friend Abel told me this story:

One day during famine time the Lord told him to walk to a remote village to hold a three-day campaign. (Do you know what a famine in Timor is like? Well, it's horrible. If we don't get enough rain in the rainy season, then the farmers can't grow a nice full crop. In the months just before harvest, January to March, we don't have any food left. The little storerooms above our kitchens are just plain empty. So we have to eat leaves off the trees like a cow or else boil the bark of a special kind of palm tree. Our stomachs are always grumbling in pain.)

Well, as soon as Abel got to the little village, he told the pastor that the Lord had sent him to there to start meetings in the pastor's tiny church right away.

"Oh, but I just can't let you," the pastor said. "You'd have to stay at my house, and I don't have any food to give you. I only have one little bowl of dry oubi to feed my whole family." (Oubi is something like a potato, only sweeter.) "If you're going to be my guest I must go on a two-day journey to find food for you first."

"Oh, don't worry about me," Abel answered. "I think it's very important that we obey the Lord, and He told me to start the meetings tonight."

"But I just can't!" The pastor was terribly upset. "I'd be a terrible host not to give you any food the whole time you were here."

(Do you know why the pastor made such a big deal out of not having enough food? It's because manners are so very important to us here in Timor. Even if a friend stops in to visit just a few minutes, the host is supposed to give him a glass of hot tea and a little something to eat, maybe a cookie or a banana. So not to feed his guest anything at all for three days—well, that was about the worst thing the poor pastor could think of.)

A real battle went on in that pastor's heart. He loved Jesus a lot and wanted to obey Him by starting the meetings, but on the other hand he was terribly embarrassed. In fact, he really felt awful. He just plain didn't know what to do.

But I believe he finally did the smartest thing possible. He had a real nice heart-to-heart talk with his heavenly Father. After telling about his problem, the pastor threw the whole mess into God's strong, capable hands. And then what a peace must have filled his heart. The Lord cared about him, and surely didn't want him to feel miserable. He'd fix everything up just right.

That night after the first meeting in the church they all came back to the pastor's house so hungry they were almost ready to faint. But then the Lord told them to do a surprising thing: He told them to heat up the little bowl of oubi even though there was only enough for two people.

It was really amazing! The pastor, his wife, all their kids, Abel, and the three other guys on the team all took a big helping. Then they took seconds and ate and ate until they were full. And since there was still some food left in the bowl when they were all done, they covered it with a cloth and went to bed.

The next morning they had a big breakfast from that same little bowl of oubi—Jesus was still multiplying the food! In fact, from that one bowl they all had three good meals each day that the revival meetings lasted.

And do you know what else the Lord Jesus did? (This just blesses my heart to pieces.) He even gave them the extra blessing of keeping the food warm for them. They never heated it again, but at breakfast the last morning it was still just as warm as it was the first time. Don't ask me how in the world the Lord did that. His power is far too wonderful to figure out or explain.

Praise the Lord, that little bowl of oubi never ran out until the meetings were finally over and the pastor was able to walk to another village twenty miles away to buy some food.

Sharing our life with Jesus, giving Him control of both the big, important areas and the insignificant ones: this is the foundation for building a Spirit-filled life. As long as we are full of self-will or stubbornness, there won't be any room for the Holy Spirit. But the more we open ourselves to the Lord, the more His love and power will be able to flow in and fill us.

The Holy Spirit is very available. All we have to do is to tell Him that we realize there are certain areas of our life that aren't under His control. The minute that we ask Him to step into those areas, take over, and fill us with Himself, He will do it. We can be sure about that, because the Bible promises, "If you then, being evil, know how to give good gifts to your children, how much more shall your Heavenly Father give the Holy Spirit to those who ask Him?" (Luke 11:13). When you ask the

Lord to fill you with the Holy Spirit, you can know by faith that He has done it.

What a beautiful process begins the moment the Holy Spirit takes possession of us. So quietly, so subtly He transforms us that we often don't realize what is happening until His work is all over. Like a gentle breeze the Holy Spirit moves deep inside, wooing us closer and closer to the Lord Jesus. He works with tenderness and deliberation, yet with unquestionable strength.

So often we prefer the mighty wind of the Holy Spirit to His gentle breeze. We would rather have a few dramatic, exciting experiences with the Lord than slowly grow into a deep, steady relationship with Him. We want the Lord to use us to do tremendous miracles, but it gets frustrating when He concentrates instead on teaching and correcting us, on slowly transforming us to become like Jesus. But the Lord knows how much we need a solid foundation. This gentle breeze must be working in our life before we'll be mature enough for His mighty wind. So let's let the gentle breeze of Jesus blow.

7

Treasures from His Storehouse

I'm sitting out here on the soft grass beside my little house writing to you. The countryside in my beloved Timor is so beautiful this afternoon.

The broad, rocky fields are usually barren and neglected; they seem to ache with a wistful loneliness. But just now they've become alive, rustling with excitement. The dull browns of their grasses have been stripped away, and now they are clothed in myriad threads of spun gold. Like little kings the grasses flutter in their gilded robes, shimmering in the glow of the late afternoon.

All around the borders of the fields lovely bamboos and coconut trees stand watching. And suddenly they too are transformed by the brilliance of the sun. All at once they are gracious queens, their lovely curves silhouetted against the shadows. Every slender leaf, every long, feathery frond has become a jewel, glistening in the sunlight, dazzling my eyes as the stately queens gently fan themselves.

And the banana trees, those funny awkward trees that usually tumble down the mountainside in a tangled clutter, have joined hands to form a procession. Their clumsy, broad leaves have been polished until they sparkle like brass, like the big brass shields of an army advancing to the front lines.

But oh, my mountains! It's my mountains that thrill me the most. They've thrown off the purple haze that usually veils them in secrecy. They've stepped out of their mystical dream world into real life. Now they are just bathed in light. It's as if the heavens had flung open their windows and all the light from the celestial city was just streaming down upon them, engulfing them, overpowering them until now they are no longer mountains but a host of mighty angels, reflecting in their magnificent faces the rich glory of the sun.

The sun. Yes, he's at the peak of his glory now. Nothing can stop him from opening wide his coffers and flinging out on the earth his golden gifts, just drenching her in a shower of his golden sundrops.

The earth has opened her heart wide to receive him. She seems thirsty for his golden light. And now there she is, glowing before me, just radiant, rapturous, as she receives such treasures from the storehouse of the sun.

You know, I believe that heaven itself has come down to Timor in this moment. That golden glory is more than just the light of the sun. It's the light of the eternal God who has come down to live and move and abide among His majestic creation.

I sit here spellbound, caught up in the splendor of the beauty all around me. But now I hear Jesus' sweet whisper in my heart: "Mel, My son, tell My beloved ones that they must follow the earth's example. Just like she receives the beautiful, golden gifts of the sun, so I long for them to open their hearts wide and take all the wonderful treasures I want to give them. When they do this, they are proving how much they love Me."

You know, my dear friend, that's really true. Of course the Lord wants us to share every part of our life with Him. But did you ever realize that He wants just as much to be able to share every part of His life with you? Right now Jesus is in heaven enjoying a fantastic life with the Father. But He wants you to enjoy it with Him. He won't be content until you are experiencing all the blessings of heaven down here on earth in your everyday life.

It's impossible for us to ever give too much of ourselves to the Lord. But did you know that it's just as impossible to take too many blessings from Him? The more we love Him the more of His beautiful treasures we'll want to receive. We really honor the Giver when we value the gifts He wants to give us.

"Oh, but Brother Mel, I don't believe you," you say. "I'm afraid that if I take too many of the Lord's blessings, I'll get proud. If I start to really enjoy life, maybe I'll forget about the Lord and run away from Him."

Well, I'm sorry to be so honest, but that's just plain ridiculous. When you take the Lord's blessings as an act of love, when you take them to make Him happy, then they'll never make you wander from Him. In fact, those nice blessings will just draw you closer than you ever were before.

I have a cute little pet monkey. He's playing around, chained to a tree just a few yards from where I'm sitting. I named him Charles Darwin.

He's a funny little guy, and usually we have to keep him tied up because we never know what mischief he'll get into next: try to pull the feathers out of the rooster's tail, chase the ducks till they squawk in terror, jump on the clothesline and ruin all our nice clean wash, eat up my favorite flower bush . . . (sometimes if he's too terribly bad I have to spank him).

But often, if I have the time to keep my eye on him, I just let Darwin run around free. I'm never afraid he'll run away to the forest to join his friends and relatives. Do you know why? My little monkey wouldn't dare leave me; he has too much to lose. He wouldn't have anyone to give him some oubi when he cries because he's hungry—or an occasional cookie if he's extra good. He wouldn't have his nice warm soapy bath once a week or his pretty blue shirt to wear. And if he ever ran away, he wouldn't have anyone to love him and pat him and give all the attention little monkeys demand.

Darwin is tied to me by a much stronger cord than his green waxy rope. He's tied by the strongest cord in the world, the cord of love and dependence, and I know that he'll never leave me.

So a good way to stay close to Jesus is to ask Him to give us everything He possibly can. You know, all these heavenly blessings were inconceivably expensive to the Lord; they are free for us, but He had to be tortured beyond endurance and finally slaughtered before He could buy them for us. He still paid the same excruciating price whether we take them or not.

It makes me sick to think of one single drop of His precious blood being wasted. I can't stand the thought of my Jesus suffering one second longer than was absolutely necessary. If He wanted me to have all these blessings so bad that He was even willing to die that awful death just to make it possible, well then the least I can do is simply to hold out my hands, open my heart, and take *everything*.

The Lord's heavenly storehouses are so jam-packed and He has such an astonishing amount of gifts to give us that it would take me ninety-seven years (talking nonstop the whole time) to tell you about all of them. But at least we have time to mention a few. I'll start with my most favorite blessing of all.

Every once in a while in these years that I've been getting to know my Best Friend, it has seemed like Jesus has stepped right out of heaven and into the very same room where I was. He'd just deluge me, overwhelm me, with His love. I'd feel His presence so strongly that I'd know without a shadow of a doubt that the Lord Jesus Christ Himself was physically right there with me.

When I first got saved I could feel Him with me all the time. Every place I went I knew that Jesus was right there beside me—whether I was walking to a nearby village to preach the gospel, eating my rice and my vegetable soup at lunchtime, or snoring in my bed sound asleep at night. Boy, it sure felt good!

I lived in a happy glow of sweetness and joy and peace like you wouldn't believe. Talk about feeling secure and content!

You'd better believe me, all I wanted to do for the rest of my life was to just live there close to my Jesus' heart.

But then one day something happened. I didn't feel His presence anymore. It seemed like Jesus had suddenly disappeared into heaven and left me there all alone, stranded and bewildered and maybe a little bit frightened. What in the world was wrong? I was really confused. It wasn't half as much fun to be a Christian if my Master wasn't with me anymore.

Boy, I'm really thankful that the God we belong to is so tenderhearted. He saw me wandering around like a little orphan feeling lonely and upset. "Mel, honey," He said to me one day, "I'm still right here with you even though you can't feel Me. You're not a little baby anymore; you're growing up. When a baby is just born, his mother has to hold him and kiss him and nurse him all the time. But when he gets a little bit bigger, she puts him down on the floor and he crawls around and plays by himself. He doesn't feel her love pats all the time anymore, but deep in his tiny heart he knows that his mamma is still with him. It would be ridiculous if that baby grew up to be a twenty-year-old man and he still had to have his mamma hug him all day to make him feel secure."

"Okay, Jesus, I get the point," I finally answered. "I guess from now on I have to learn to live by faith." So that's what I tried to do for the next few months. I had to preach a lot of sermons at myself: *Mel, even if you feel rotten Jesus is still right here . . . . Mel, quit listening to your emotions. It's a fact that the Lord is with you . . . . Mel, living by faith means hanging onto the truth no matter what. So get busy and do it!*

But one day I got so homesick for Jesus' presence I just couldn't stand it. It was fine to walk by faith, but that really couldn't compare with the joy of that sweet fellowship I used to know. So once again my dear heavenly Father took pity on me.

That day I happened to be in the little village of Nifukani with my team. We were having a morning prayer meeting in the church, and my brother-in-law Bu Franz was leading the devotions. He was talking about Elijah being caught up to heaven in a fiery chariot.

And all of a sudden it seemed like heaven itself came bursting down upon me. Just wave after wave of glory and pure love flooded through my being. I was swimming in it, soaking in it. And my Jesus was so close to me that I could feel His nearness all around me and inside of me. I could actually feel Him right against my skin. He was touching me physically, and oh, it felt so beautiful that I thought I was going to burst.

It was as if He had wrapped a mantle of His love around my body. I was drunk with the intensity of His presence. For at least ten minutes I tingled all over. I was so still I couldn't move, and I felt like I was going to faint.

Gradually, that overpowering feeling went away. But in its place it left an assurance so strong that nothing in this world can ever shake it: I have personally come into the presence of God, He will never leave me, and I never have to leave this holy place of oneness with Him.

But the most precious part of that experience is that it's not over yet. I have never lost the wonderful feeling that the Lord is with me. Oh, it's a lot less intense now, but it's still just as real and just as close and precious. Right this very minute I can sense the mighty, yet gentle, arms of Jesus around me.

Of course, I know by faith that He's holding me in His love; I don't need any nice feelings to prove that to me. It's a fact that I know in my mind and in my heart. But the wonderful part is that I can actually feel it too.

I really wish that you too, wherever you are right now, could experience the blessing of feeling His wonderful presence right there with you. I believe the Lord wants every single one of His children to have that privilege (Ephesians 3:17-19, Living Bible). That's one of the blessings He died in order to give us. He doesn't want our Christian life to be dreary and lonely. He wants each one of us to know the sheer wonder and delight of actually feeling His love.

Please believe me—I'm not a special case! He wants to make Himself just as real to you as He has to me, although of course He might do it in a different way.

But there's one little problem. The Lord's blessings are free, but that doesn't necessarily mean they're within easy reach. Almost always we have to make a real effort to take them. If we're going to really live in His presence, there isn't any shortcut—we have to be willing to spend a lot of time alone with Him. We have to take time for Jesus. (Actually, in this busy, hectic world, our time is the most valuable gift we can give Him.)

We have to be willing to really get quiet inside so that we can start to feel His love. We'll never feel it if we just rush through our fifteen-minute devotion time in the morning and send Him a few quick prayers during the day. This gift of His presence is far too valuable for the Lord to give us if we're not willing to spend time seeking Him.

But, my friend, if you do know in your heart that you want Jesus more than anything else in the world and that you want Him to reveal His love to you so that you can feel it, just tell Him that right now. Ask Him to give you this wonderful blessing and to make your heart ready to receive it, because He surely wants to.

Now the Lord Jesus is a very practical guy. He wants to make your body feel just as good as your spirit does. He knows that as long as your body is sick you're going to feel miserable, and as long as you're feeling miserable you can't fully appreciate His love.

So if you're sick right now, I have a very special message for you: The Lord Jesus wants to heal you! Your Jesus, who loves you and cares for you so deeply, does not want you to be tormented by sickness.

Let me read you a beautiful Bible verse. It expresses the Lord's heart's desire for you at this moment: "Beloved, I pray that in all respects you may prosper and be in good health, just as your soul prospers" (3 John 2). You might be longing that the Lord would heal you. But I tell you with all my heart that *Jesus wants to heal you far more than you want to be healed.* He is yearning to set His power loose in your life to make you every bit whole.

(There are some rare cases when it is the Lord's perfect will for someone to suffer with a physical problem. But that's only because He knows that the infirmity will actually draw the person much closer to Him and enable him to experience more of the abundant life than he ever could have otherwise.

(If this is the Lord's will for you, then your infirmity would be a supreme honor, a beautiful proof of His love. But if you find yourself complaining about your sickness, if you think of it as your "thorn in the flesh" or your "cross," and if deep in your heart you really want to be healed, then I don't think the Lord wants you to be sick. He wants to heal you.)

Maybe you're saying to yourself right now, *Well, if Jesus wants to heal me so bad and I'm still not healed, what's the matter? Maybe it's my fault. Maybe I don't have enough faith.*

I've seen lots of precious sick people condemn themselves to pieces. They get so nervous about what they are doing wrong that the healing couldn't possibly get through to them no matter how hard it tried.

Your job is to keep reminding yourself how much He cares about you. Really rest your heart on the sweet fact that you are so important to Him that He wants to heal you. You know, when your whole being is quiet, just resting in the Lord, it will be easy for His healing power to flow into your body.

When Jesus was on earth, He had an extra-special place in His heart for sick people. And He's still the same today. One of His favorite ways of proving to somebody that He loves them is by healing their body. One day in 1973, for example, He sent one of my friends, a lady named Ibu Marow, to the village of Meo to pray for the sick people. And before she left town a few days later He had healed all twenty-seven of the people she had prayed for.

Meo is a charming little village, typical of all the villages in

127

Timor. In the very center you'll find two long palm houses with shaggy grass roofs. They probably look like big barns where all the neighborhood cows and pigs ought to live. But they aren't. They're the schoolhouse and the church.

All the little palm huts aren't arranged in neat rows around them like you might expect. Oh, no, they're scattered over the side of the mountain facing every which way as if one day, when God was in a playful mood, He tossed a bunch of little brown pebbles over the brow of the cliff. And there those little pebbles sit, nestled between big boulders and swallowed up by the long, swishing grass. It's hard to tell where the grass leaves off and their roofs begin; their walls are no more than a row of slender trees planted tightly together, I think, bound by strong cord from the wild grass to make a shelter from the sun. Those huts were planted there on the wild, free hillside; they grew along with the billowing grass. It seems like they were born the day the world began, for nature has claimed them as her own and skillfully blended them into the beautiful life of the mountainside.

But life in the mountains isn't always beautiful. Sometimes it is rough and mean. And those little huts, for all their charming sweetness, are crudely simple. They don't have much to offer in the way of comfort—a dank, dirty floor, and meager, wobbling furniture chopped from the hills nearby. The bed, for instance, is nothing more than four notched sticks stuck in the dirt in the shape of a bed, with longer poles lying in the notches to form a frame. Rough planks have been thrown here and there across these poles. And over the planks, scratchy palm leaves make an excuse for a sheet. There is no pillow except for a small log placed at the head of the bed. The poor little bed crouches there in the dark room of the hut, trying its best to balance a sleeping body in its flimsy support.

And those little palm walls—they are no match for the cruel wind. Without even a struggle he comes plunging through the cracks at night, twisting like a knife into the bodies of the

villagers. They have no blankets. What can they do to try
to shield themselves from him? They build a fire on the floor in
the middle of their house, and very soon the smoke emerges
like another monster to smother them. Choking for air, they
huddle as close to the fire as possible, trying to keep their toes
from burning and their backs from freezing.

In one of these huts a man named Stefanus Toto lived. For
him, his house had become a grimy prison. He couldn't run
outside in the morning to take a deep breath of the sweet air.
He couldn't see the smile of the sun or hear the songs of the
happy daytime breezes. You see, Stefanus was paralyzed.

The poor guy had to lie on that awful scratchy bed all day.
He couldn't move and he couldn't talk. In fact, he couldn't do
anything for himself. His wife and little kids had to feed him
and bathe him and try to keep him from being horribly
depressed. But that was next to impossible. Poor Stefanus
couldn't even get to the bathroom when he needed to; he just
had to wet the bed. And pretty soon his room smelled like—
well, to be honest, it smelled like an outhouse.

Can you imagine anybody being so miserable? The poor guy
had been like that for four whole years. He hadn't gotten off
his bed that whole time. Well, I think Jesus couldn't stand to
see His precious son suffer like that. That's why He finally
sent His faithful servant, Ibu Marow, to Meo to minister to him.

And one sparkly Sunday afternoon she walked into his
sickroom, laid her hands on his head, and said a simple,
uncomplicated prayer: "Dear Jesus, I know You don't want
Stefanus to be sick like this. Please heal him. We know You
have the power, and we know You are going to use it to help
Stefanus. Thank You that You are going to give him a brand
new wonderful life. Amen."

But Jesus in His wonderful wisdom didn't heal him right
away. He knew Stefanus needed a good, deep sleep first. So
that night for the first time in months he slept like a contented
little baby. Sometime during the night, while his whole being

was relaxed, God's magnificent power entered his body and devoured the paralysis. It drove out every trace of the disease. Stefanus was totally healed.

When he woke up, all of a sudden it dawned on him that he felt tremendous! Something wonderful had happened. Gingerly he sat up. Then pretty soon he got brave enough to swing his legs over the side of the bed. And before he knew it, he had gotten out of bed all by himself and was walking toward the door, free from his horrible dungeon forever. Praise the Lord!

He walked around the house all day, his face wrinkled into a huge, happy smile. He couldn't quit thanking God for the new life he felt in his body. By the next Sunday he was strong enough to walk all the way to church and give a beautiful testimony about the power and love of his God.

8

More Treasures from Jesus

Jo Daniel is a beautiful girl. Her golden brown eyes are always twinkling with fun, and her fat black braids bounce merrily on her shoulders as she skips down the streets of Soe. She's the kind of girl who always has a circle of friends around her. She loves to laugh and sing and make other people happy with her sunny personality.

Jo is my pastor's daughter; I've known her ever since she was a tiny girl. When the revival started, she was only ten years old. She was one of the first little kids to join the children's teams that went out witnessing all over our area. She was on the team that got in trouble when they disobeyed Jesus by climbing the tree to eat the guavas. Do you remember that story from *Like a Mighty Wind?* The angels stuck their clothes up in the top of the tree, and they couldn't get them down until they had repented.

Jo and her team also got to watch Jesus deliver a pagan priest from the power of Satan. After the service where the little kids had been preaching, the Lord told them to go to a certain witch doctor's house and pray that he'd be delivered from all the demons that had been controlling him. Well, the Lord did deliver him all right. But all the demons inside of him came out of his mouth in the form of a long black snake about one inch in diameter. When the kids saw the snake, they got so scared they all ran out of the house. Their team leader had to really yell at them before they got enough nerve to come back inside. By the time they entered the house, the snake had disappeared.

Now I'm sure that the man hadn't had a real snake living in his stomach. But the Lord just made those demons take that visible form to teach the little kids how very real the power of Satan is.

Well, Jo isn't a little girl anymore. In the summer of 1973 she was living in Kupang with her relatives while she went to the big high school nearby. One night after school she went to her girlfriend's house for a little visit. All the girls there happened to be playing with a *Jailangkung,* the Indonesian form of a Ouija board. (A *Jailangkung* is actually a basket with several sticks in it. A piece of string is tied to the end of each stick. But one of the sticks also has a piece of chalk tied to the other end of the string.)

The girls first called in spirits (evil spirits) to help them. Then they asked the basket a question about something they didn't know, for example, "Where is my lost pencil?" And the chalk, without any human help at all, jumped to a chalkboard lying beside the basket and wrote out the answer: "Under your bed." Of course this whole thing is horribly demonic. But the girls didn't see anything wrong with it; they were just having fun.

Late that night Jo ran back to her house to go to bed. But all of a sudden while she was sleeping, she had a horrible attack from Satan. She started to moan and shake and sweat. Her aunt and uncle woke up immediately. When they felt her forehead, it was burning hot, and they figured that she'd been struck by an awful malarial fever.

They called the doctor, and he gave her several malaria shots, but they didn't help a bit. Nothing helped. Several days went by and Jo got worse and worse. She was delirious by now, saying all kinds of wild things that didn't make any sense at all. Either she'd toss in her bed moaning as if in a terrible fear or she'd lie brooding and morosely silent, unable to say a word.

132

After two weeks Pastor Daniel finally decided to bring his sick daughter back to Soe. They bundled her into a jeep and brought her up the mountain. But Jo just huddled in her corner in a terrified silence. When I went to my pastor's house to visit her, she didn't even recognize me; she just mumbled some incoherent words I couldn't understand. I couldn't believe my eyes. Was this the same sweet Jo who used to wave at me from far down the street and come running up to say hi? I got really concerned.

But praise the Lord, it wasn't too hard a case for Jesus to handle. One of our most faithful team members, Susana, who was staying at the pastor's house, began to fast and pray for her. The Lord quickly revealed what was causing the trouble: demon powers from that *Jailangkung* game were torturing her mind.

So Pastor Daniel and Susana rebuked the devil and commanded him to leave Jo alone. Then they committed her into the loving hands of Jesus, asking Him to soothe her and plant His healing peace deep in her heart.

And the Lord did just what they had asked. He quieted her mind by chasing away all her tormenting thoughts and dissolving her fears. He gave her His thoughts of peace instead.

I went to visit Jo a few days later, and I was thrilled to see her walking around the house, smiling and laughing, her same sunny self again. Jesus had completely healed her.

Now actually this story leads me right into my next subject. Jo needed the Lord Jesus to heal her, but she also needed Him to free her from the devil's torment. As you can see, neither of those things was a bit hard for Jesus to do. He has total power to heal us, and He also has total power over the devil.

You and I must never ever underestimate our God's tremendous power. Like I said before, nothing, absolutely nothing, is impossible for Him to do. The Lord Jesus Christ has *infinitely* greater power than the devil. He is the devil's Master, and whether he likes it or not, Satan *must* obey our almighty Jesus.

My friend, I tell you with all my heart that if our lives are right with the Lord and if we're living under the shelter of His blood, we have *no reason at all* to be afraid of the devil. The Bible says he can't even touch us, let alone hurt us (1 John 5:18).

I'd like to tell you about one of the most magnificent demonstrations of the Lord's power (and also one of the most horrifying acts of Satan) I've ever seen. For a long time I wondered, "Now should I tell you this or shouldn't I?" It's possible that you'll think I had a bad dream one night and made all this up myself. But I didn't. It is the truth.

In Timor there are certain people we call the Alauts, and of all the pagan people left in Timor the Alauts are the most deeply feared. They have reached the highest peak of demon possession, and their practices are even more dreadful than those of voodooism.

They actually go through a special ceremony where they put their whole being under Satan's control. They give themselves to him totally. They get so filled with his evil power that somehow they are able to separate their spirit from their soul and body for the purpose of killing their enemies.

At night the Alaut will go to bed as if everything were normal. But when the whole village has quieted down and is asleep, he will begin his horrible work. Using a certain fetish, maybe a root or a special stone to help him accomplish this, he will command his spirit to leave his body and go to the house of his enemy. (Often the Alaut's spirit will "ride" to the house on the back of a night owl. When the villagers hear the owl's eerie cry at night, they will lie frozen on their beds, shuddering in terror, wondering if the spirit is coming for them.)

Once he's at the house, the Alaut's spirit will put a spell over his enemy, making him fall into a deep sleep so that he can't wake up until the filthy job is finished. The Alaut uses a special demonic knife—it's a real, tangible knife about two inches long, but it's so dull that without supernatural power it could never cut anything. With this knife he makes an incision in his victim's belly. He cuts out just a little corner of his liver, or if he's extra-vicious, half of it, or even the whole thing. Sometimes he will even go so far as to stuff dead leaves in the area where the liver used to be. After closing the enemy up, the spirit of the Alaut goes back home with a visible piece of human liver. During the night it expands to about ten times its original size.

The next morning after the Alaut wakes up, he will boil it in a special clay pot used only for that purpose and eat it for breakfast. The way he cooks it will determine whether the enemy will only get sick or whether he will die. If the pot of liver boils over, the enemy will die. Alauts usually take their victim's liver, because it is supposedly the most delicious human organ to eat. But sometimes they will open up a pregnant mother and cut out a part of her unborn baby—its hand or leg or ear—and eat that for breakfast.

It's obvious why the Alauts are so greatly feared. The slightest offense will put someone on their blacklist. If one of them walked up to his neighbor and said, "Oh, that's a nice shirt you're wearing; can I have it?" and the neighbor said no, that would be enough excuse for the Alaut to consider him an enemy. (The Alaut's power will only work on someone who has supposedly offended him.)

Before the revival started, there were thousands of these Alauts in Timor. As you can see, the Holy Spirit surely didn't pick an easy place to start the Indonesian revival! There was no way to control these demon-possessed people. The police were far too afraid to arrest them; they knew the whole mob of Alauts would turn against them and butcher them for sure. There was only one way people could get protection—to become an Alaut themselves. Even the pastors of some churches had become Alauts in self-defense.

This whole story would be far too gruesome for me to believe if I hadn't seen with my own two eyes the horrible utensils the Alauts use—the small, demonic knife and the bloody cooking pot where they boil the human liver. When I saw the Alauts themselves, I could easily tell that they were terribly controlled by the power of Satan. Some of them were so filthy that they obviously never took a bath. Their hair was matted and greasy, and their eyes were all red and bloodshot—just horrible to look at. Looking at them was like looking into the face of Satan.

I've slept in the villages of the Alauts dozens of times. When the Lord told us to go there to preach in their villages, our friends told us we were crazy—we'd never come back alive. The devil in the Alauts would hate us for invading his territory and he'd turn his power full-force against us. But trusting in the protection of the blood of Jesus, we obeyed the Lord and went to those villages anyway.

Many nights we heard all kinds of strange noises outside our door. We knew the spirits of the Alauts were trying to get in to kill us. But the Lord must have sent a host of angels to surround our house, because not a single demon could ever get in.

The Lord gave us far more than just protection from the enemy; He gave us the power to cast out demons in His name. He gave us the power to go on the offensive against Satan and win an overwhelming victory.

We'd walk into those demon-infested villages to hold meetings as the Lord had told us to, and because they knew the gospel was the only hope of breaking the Alauts' power, the village elders would order every one in the nearby area to come to the meeting. And praise the Lord, the sheer power of the Word of God was able to do what nothing else ever could; it slashed through those Alauts' filthy black hearts and brought them face-to-face with the truth that they needed to repent.

I tell you, it was one of the greatest thrills of my life to watch those wicked Alauts renounce their sinful life and turn to Jesus. (If the Lord can save them, He can save anybody!) I saw the Lord miraculously deliver them from the grip of Satan, setting them totally free from their sins and the power of the devil. I personally have seen my Jesus deliver *hundreds* of these Alauts.

(But it was a real struggle to cast the demons out of some of them. They were so full of lying spirits that it often took hours to get them to admit their sin. I remember how grateful I felt during those long sessions for the gifts of the Spirit. Without the Lord's supernatural wisdom and discernment, I don't think we ever could have brought those people through to victory.)

When the Lord saved them, He did a total job. They became different people. Of course they burned their fetishes and all their demonic utensils. They turned their backs on their old way of life. Even their physical appearance changed. They cleaned themselves up. Their eyes lost that horribly wicked look and became bright and sparkly. And their faces, which once had been so ugly I couldn't stand to look at them, shone with the lovely joy of Jesus. Of all the Christians I have ever met, they were the most radiant and the most beautiful.

I remember one old lady in particular. She was about seventy years old, and she had killed more than one hundred people in that awful way I just told you about. It was so precious to see her cry for joy the night she was delivered. Tears of gratitude were streaming down her face when she said, "Oh, I'm so thankful to my Jesus for saving me, or pretty soon now I'd be in hell!"

But those dear former Alauts didn't just sit around enjoying their salvation. They turned themselves totally over to the Lord so that He possessed them as completely as the devil had before. And filled with His mighty Holy Spirit, they went all over the area telling everyone about their wonderful Redeemer and His wonderful power to change lives.

If Jesus can deliver those people from Satan, He can certainly deliver you. My friend, the devil has no right whatsoever to torment you. You do not have to live under his oppression. You do not have to be depressed or live in a dark, dreary world. You do not have to be held in bondage to fear or sin. *Jesus died to set you free!*

The devil is a thief, a bloody, mean thief. He wants to destroy you and to twist and ruin your life. By every means possible He is trying to steal away the beautiful new life the Lord longs to give you. But by his death Jesus paid the ransom fee to deliver you from every bit of Satan's power. It makes Him fiercely angry when the devil tries to snatch you back, and He is not going to tolerate it. He wants to set you free!

So—Satan, in the almighty name of Jesus, I come against you. I command you to get your filthy hands off my friend's life. No longer can you torment or oppress him. You cannot hold him in bondage in any way. Jesus shed His precious blood to set him free! So from this moment on, your dominion over my friend is finished.

And Lord Jesus, I commit my friend into Your precious loving hands. Let him know he is completely protected. Let him know that You have placed the fiery wall of Your presence and truth around him, and no demon of hell can touch his life again. Thank You that You bought our victory with Your blood. You have the power to guarantee us complete and total victory when we come against the devil in Your name. Amen.

The delight of feeling Jesus' presence, healing for your body, complete deliverance from Satan—these are just a few of the heavenly blessings the Lord longs for you to experience. There are so many more. I want to list some of them for you, but please do me a favor. Don't skip over this list and hop ahead to find the next story. Instead, think about each blessing and try to figure out how the Holy Spirit could make it become a reality in your life.

This is what the Lord wants to give you:

The joy of knowing your sins are forgiven (Ephesians 1:7; 1 John 1:9).

Protection when you have to walk alone in a big city in the dark (Psalm 91).

Salvation for your entire family (even your hippie son who's on drugs) (Acts 16:31; Isaiah 54:13).

A happy marriage (Ephesians 5:21-33).

Rest from your tensions so you can really relax (Psalm 23:2; Matthew 11:28-30).

Grace so you can love your boss no matter what (2 Corinthians 9:8).

Wisdom to know when to spank your kids and when to hug them, or to know which job you should take (Ephesians 1:9; James 1:5).

The security of knowing you are deeply loved (Ephesians 3:17; Romans 8:38,39).

Strength to do your housework (Philippians 4:13).

A beautiful joy that keeps your heart singing all day long (Psalm 34:1; 1 Peter 1:8).

A good sleep at night (Psalm 127:2; 4:8).

Victory so you don't have to lose your temper (Romans 8:1,2; Jude 24).

The knowledge that God is well-pleased with you (Ephesians 1:6; Isaiah 62:3-5; Song of Soloman 4:7).

The tender comfort of God when your little baby dies (2 Corinthians 1:3-5; 2 Thessalonians 2:16,17).

The privilege of suffering for Jesus and discovering His overwhelming sweetness (Philippians 1:29; Romans 8:17,18).

A special ministry of your own so you can know the joy of working with the Lord (I Corinthians 3:9).

The thrill of knowing Jesus face-to-face (Ephesians 1:17,18; 3:19).

Since the Lord has so much scheduled for you on His heavenly agenda, I'm going to suggest that you make a little appointment with the Holy Spirit. Sometime soon sit down together—just the two of you, with your Bible. Ask Him to show you what is lacking in your life—which parts of the abundant life you still haven't experienced. You know, even if we have been walking with Jesus for fifty years, there is always more that He wants to give us. I know I still need a lot more in my life.

For too long we've been making excuses for our poverty-stricken Christian lives. "Oh, but we must be realistic," we tell ourselves. "The Christian life has its defeats and failures as well as its victories. We just can't be perfect, and life can't always be abundant." Of course life has its defeats! We won't have a perfect life until we get to heaven.

But actually, I think we get so comfortable with our same old little problems that we aren't willing to make the effort to let the Lord change us. Jesus has the solution to *every* problem in this life. He wants us to experience the same complete victory He had when He lived on earth. Now don't get me wrong. I'm not saying we're not supposed to have any problems. Jesus Himself had some fierce, nasty ones. But He was so filled with the Spirit that He had the power to live above them. And this should be our goal.

So if we're really honest today, we'll come to the Holy Spirit and ask Him to exchange our problems with His heavenly blessings. We'll quit watering down the Bible; we'll take all of those marvelous promises literally, for ourselves. We'll ask the Holy Spirit to flood our lives in a new way so that He can bring us into a fresh, exciting dimension in our walk with Jesus.

9

A New Kind of Kingdom

The sun was already flooding the hillside with gold, setting the red of the poppies on fire. The little olive trees danced for joy as the sundrops splashed through their leafy fingers and collected in golden puddles on the ground below.

Jesus sat up and rubbed His eyes. Gentle little breezes kissed Him on the face, and the friendly morning lilies waved at Him from their beds under the trees. Jesus smiled. The world was wide-awake, already bursting out in a harmonious cantata of praise to the Creator. He took a deep, cool drink of the mountain air and whispered, "Oh, thank you, Father! Another beautiful day to live with You!"

All around Him the disciples lay huddled in their robes fast asleep. *This will never do,* thought Jesus to Himself. So He reached over and gave Philip and Andrew a playful poke in the ribs.

"Come on, you guys. It's time to get up. Let's get some breakfast going." Philip moaned and rolled over. Pretty soon he gave a huge, rumbling yawn . . . .

Half an hour later they were seated around the campfire munching on some figs and olives, some boiled pike (that James and John had caught the day before), and some home-made cornbread (fresh from Mrs. Peter's oven).

All of a sudden the peaceful breakfast exploded into a fight. Matthew glared angrily at Nathanael. "You idiot! What makes you think you're so big anyway? Why should you be vice-president in the new Kingdom? I am a lot smarter than all of you dum-dums put together. Why, I'm just tremendous at math. I can multiply and divide in my head—"

"Big deal!" Simon Zealotes couldn't stand it any longer. "Brains ain't everything! When it comes to courage and zeal, I make the rest of you guys look sick. Why, I could whip a whole Roman legion—if I only had a sword, that is."

"Boy, are you a bunch of dumb jerks!" Thomas exploded. "Common sense should tell you that *I* am the one to be vice-president; after all, I am the most logical—"

"But one thing's certain," snarled Judas, his green eyes flashing. "I'll make a terribly good secretary of the treasury!"

"Oh, shut up, you stupid nuts!" yelled Peter as he punched Judas in the stomach. "Of course *I'll* get the best position. I'm the Master's best friend. He tells me all His secrets, doesn't He? . . ."

Jesus gave a long, patient sigh. "Oh, no, not this again," He muttered to Himself. As soon as there was a slight lull, He broke in. "I must have told you guys this ten times by now, but I'll try to explain it again.

"My Kingdom is not an earthly kingdom. It has a whole different set of values. If you were *really* the greatest, you wouldn't care what position you got. You'd want to *serve* the rest of us. You'd want to be the janitor, not the vice-president. In My Kingdom the ones who have love and kindness and humility get the greatest honors."

Yes, Jesus has called us to the Kingdom of love. And in order to be a part of that Kingdom, love must reign supreme in our hearts. It has to be the standard that governs our every motive and action.

But brother, those poor disciples sure had the whole thing screwed up. They still hadn't gotten it through their thick heads what Jesus' life of love was all about. And maybe you and I are sometimes just as bad off as they were.

What are we supposed to do if we are going to really love each other? Well, I think we should simply have the same attitude toward one another that God has toward us. He thinks we're valuable and sees an awful lot of potential in us. Right? So then we should feel the same way; one of the first laws in the Kingdom of love is to realize that each of us has a whole lot of fantastic qualities imbedded in us—somewhere. (Maybe they're buried and we can't see them, but they're still there.)

Let's just pretend that there is a lady at your church named Mrs. Smith. She's very active in the ladies' missionary club, and she always cooks the fanciest chicken for the church suppers, but still nobody likes her. You see, Mrs. Smith has a big mouth. She's always criticizing somebody, and some of the things she has said about the pastor's wife are downright nasty. To make matters worse, Mrs. Smith is very crabby; it seems like she's always in a bad mood, and she makes everybody uncomfortable if they have to stick around her too long.

Now how can the royal law of love apply here? Well, I believe we have to look beyond Mrs. Smith's faults, her sharp tongue and crabbiness, and see the beautiful qualities in her personality that have never been able to get developed. If Mrs. Smith is interested in church work, then maybe she's basically a very friendly person and would like to help others if she just knew the right way to go about it. She obviously is also a talented woman since she's such a good cook. So we agree that Mrs. Smith is a wonderful person; she has some great qualities. Now what? Well, another law of love is to realize that she's also unique. There's never been a single person like her before in the whole world. No other person has her particular combination of character and personality traits, hang-ups, abilities, and physical appearance. She's an original, impossible to copy, so that makes her very valuable, right? Then we'd better respect her. We'd better not take her for granted—and we'd better make sure we never despise her—but rather treat her like the valuable human being she is.

We know she's a wonderful person and we respect her individuality, but now *we have to do something about it*. Now we're getting down to the nitty-gritty, and here's where the fun begins.

Where should we start? Well, real love always tries to meet the need of the loved one. So we'll have to keep our eyes wide-open, hunting for any clues about what type of need Mrs. Smith has. That shouldn't be too hard. If we make an effort to be friendly to her and try to get to know her better, it won't be long before we find out that the poor lady has a real problem with depression. No matter what she does, she can never seem to shake it; that's what makes her so crabby. In Christian love we'll bring her problem to Jesus and ask Him to give us wisdom to know how she can be cured.

Maybe your daughter has a different need than Mrs. Smith's. She doesn't have enough self-confidence and needs a lot of encouragement to make her appreciate herself. So as her concerned parent you'll let her know all the things you like about her. You'll be sensitive to her feelings and try to build her up instead of knock her down.

But your Sunday School teacher may have a different type of need altogether. He might have the practical kind. So you might end up baby-sitting all his kids for free, just so he and his wife can go off on a date and have a lot of fun alone without the kids to bother them. (By the way, this practical kind of love is what the Spirit-filled life is all about.)

Love doesn't stop with meeting the loved one's needs, though; it also tries to do a whole bunch of nice, thoughtful little things to make the person happy. Real love means being friendly and considerate. So it would be a good idea to tell your college roommate that that particular shade of yellow in her dress looks gorgeous with her red hair (if you can say that without telling a lie, that is). And it would be really nice of you to drive your boss to a baseball game, possibly even paying for his ticket, since he's such a baseball fan. I'm sure your mother would be thrilled to death if you'd clean up the kitchen for her after supper, since she's tired out from working so hard to cook a nice meal.

Love really cares about the other person's feelings and tries to see the situation from their point of view. When your secretary bursts into your office stomping, angry, very upset because she can't have the three days off to spend with her sailor boyfriend who is home on leave, the Christian thing to do would be to listen sympathetically. When she's let off all her steam, tactfully explain how much you need her help, but then, if it's possible, make arrangements to have her days off switched around. Don't you think that would be a lot nicer than firing her?

Let's pretend that some evening when your husband comes home from work, the first thing he does after sticking his head in the door is to yell, "This house is a mess! What have you done all day?" When you finally get the meal on the table he grunts, "Oh, ick! Meat loaf again? Why can't you think of anything new?" Now if you'll just stop and think for a moment instead of snapping back, you'll realize that he's grouchy because he's tired and has had a rough day at work. He's not really disgusted with you. This might shock him, but next time he comes home from work, treat him like a king instead of like an overworked slave. Tell him how much you appreciate him, and do everything in your power to make him comfortable and happy. You can prove your love to him by being understanding and by figuring out why he does or says things the way he does.

Let's pretend that someone you know has a habit that bugs you to death—your brother, for instance. He chews his fingernails until they're ragged, bleeding stumps. But since you love him you'll realize that maybe he doesn't even notice what he's doing; he has no idea how much chewing his fingernails grates on your nerves. In that case, you'd better tell him! But if he just can't help it, if for some crazy reason he's addicted to his fingernails, the only thing you can do is pray for him. But maybe Jesus wants to help you instead of him; maybe the Lord wants to give you this grace so your brother doesn't bother you so much.

Now if, by any stretch of the imagination, you and your parents ever end up in an argument—or have a strong difference of opinion (maybe that's a "more spiritual" thing to call it)—the Lord Jesus would be really proud of you if you'd try to listen to what they're telling you. He wants to help you figure out why they feel the way they do about the situation. He wants you to see it through their eyes. That's one way you can prove your love both to the Lord and to your parents—by not being so stuck on your own important feelings or opinions that you're blind and deaf to theirs.

Occasionally love means being mature enough to not take things personally. So when your neighbor lady, Mrs. Jones, backs out of her driveway and runs over your lovely garden, demolishing your prized rosebush, you'd better realize she didn't do it on purpose; she's just sort of clumsy. And in order to stay friends with her, maybe you'd better build a fence.

One of the most important aspects of love is accepting others just the way they are. This means we don't try to change them. If that needs to be done, then we'll let the Lord take care of it. Instead of expecting other people to adjust to us, we'll try to adjust ourselves to them. If your pastor, for example, is always cracking jokes in the middle of his Sunday morning sermon and you think he ought to be more dignified, you'd better make up your mind that you're going to get used to it. Instead of making a big fuss about it to the elders, or getting so disgusted that you leave the church, realize that the Lord Himself has a tremendous sense of humor. Just decide that you're going to be thankful that the pastor's sermons are lively instead of dry, as long as you have to sit through them. Pretty soon I bet you'll be laughing at his jokes along with everyone else.

Before we go on, I want to make one more comment about the royal law of love. If we're going to love people the way the Lord Jesus wants us to, then we should overlook their weak points and spend our time thinking about their good qualities. That's what the Bible means when it says, "Love covers a multitude of sins" (I Peter 4:8). So next time your best friend gets in a bad mood and he doesn't want to talk to anybody, including you, just concentrate on how much fun it is to be with him when he's in a good mood. Remind yourself that it's his artistic temperament, which helps do such nice creative things, that also makes him feel so down in the dumps sometimes. So try to stick it out and be his friend no matter what.

Okay, so much for that. That part is the nice, fun side of love. It gets a lot more sticky to love somebody when they're bad, when they make a horrible mess out of their life, when they just plain sin.

As a human being our first reaction when someone falls into sin is to condemn them. We draw our holy robes around us, stick our nose up in the air, and think we're really spiritual when we say, "Boy, the Lord is really going to punish them! They sure need it bad!"

Now number one, it's not very nice for us to act like the judge. That's the Lord's department. We make His job a lot harder, and we actually damage the person when we criticize them. God's desire is always to draw the sinner back into close fellowship with Himself. But when we criticize, we just drive the poor guy away in the opposite direction. Our only job is to love and forgive him and let God figure out how to deal with him about his sin.

And number two, it's ridiculous for us to judge others, because we're really not smart enough. Only God is smart enough to take all the facts into consideration and come up with the right verdict.

He has perfect wisdom. He knows when the guilty guy needs a good hard spanking to make him wake up and realize that what he's doing is wrong.

But the Lord also knows that for some people this approach

would never work at all. It would just make them more rebellious than ever. So instead of spanking those guys (sending difficult circumstances into their life), He throws His arms around them and just blesses and blesses them until they can't stand it anymore. They drop their sin in a hurry and come running back to the shelter of His forgiveness and mercy. For those guys, it's the *goodness* of the Lord, not the punishment, that leads them to repentance (Romans 2:4).

Now I'm a prime example of this. When I was a little boy, I wasn't the perfect little angel you might have expected I'd be. No, I was very naughty. In fact, to be dead honest with you, I was a real brat.

Mamma really had her hands full with me. I was stubborn and rebellious and I always wanted my own way. In fact, I actually thought I was the king of the house and everybody, mamma and papa included, ought to obey me when I told them what to do.

Wow! Was I ever a big bully! One of my favorite tricks was to steal the meat off my little brothers' and sisters' plates. While papa was asking the blessing before the meal and everybody else had their eyes shut like they were supposed to, I'd grab the meat, stuff it in my mouth and swallow it real quick before papa reached the amen.

When the little kids saw that their favorite part of the meal was gone, they'd all start to cry. Of course everybody knew who did it. But none of them dared to make too big of a fuss at me, because then I'd take revenge—and usually that was far worse.

Lots of times I'd get mad at mamma. Don't ask me why. She was always a very sweet and nice mamma. But I'd get mad at her anyway. I figured the best way to get even was to give her a big scare.

So I'd take her big kitchen knife and go out to her favorite watermelon patch. I'd hide there under the leaves and have an all-day feast. Boy, I tell you, those watermelons were really good—it still makes my mouth water just to think about them. I'd eat and eat until my tummy was so fat and round it was almost ready to pop, and then I'd curl up in a ball and take a long nap.

Well, by the time it got to be sundown and there was still no sign of little Mel, mamma was frantic. "Mel, oh, Mel, where are you? Where are you, honey?" I could hear her calling in the field on the other side of the house. I think she had visions of me falling into the ravine, my body splattered on the rocks below.

"Oh, Mel, honey, mamma loves you. I shouldn't have yelled at you this morning. It was wrong of me to say you are naughty. You're a very dear little boy . . . ."

That's what I had been waiting for all day: for mamma to repent of accusing me falsely. After I saw that she was good and sorry, I'd casually pop out of the melon patch and say, "Hi, mamma, is supper ready? Hurry up, let's go eat."

But sometimes I was even worse than that. I remember once, after a good hard spanking (which I'm sure I really needed), I decided to play the you-killed-me act. So I lay face down in the middle of the dining-room dirt floor and didn't move. When suppertime came, everyone politely stepped over me to get to the table. "Don't bother him," they told each other. "He'll get over it in an hour or two when he's hungry."

But they had underestimated little Mel's abilities to act like the world's stubbornest mule when he wanted to get his own way. Do you know, I actually lay there on that dirt floor for two whole days, without eating, without even moving a muscle!

Finally my ever-loving, tenderhearted mamma just couldn't stand it any longer. As she gently picked me up in her arms and asked me to forgive her, there were tears in her eyes. But I'm sure there was a gleam of triumph in mine. I knew that once again I had come out on top.

Not too long after that I'm pretty sure that papa, mamma, and the Lord had a little conference with each other. They all agreed that it was hopeless to train me with spankings and lectures. That would just make me so stubborn that hell itself couldn't budge me.

The only alternative was love; when I was bad, they would just love me to death. And I tell you, they really hit on it that time. They couldn't have chosen a more effective weapon. Their love worked like a sledge hammer in my heart and just broke it all to pieces.

For instance, if I'd beat up my little brother Ias until his shirt was ripped and his cheeks were swollen and bloody, instead of getting upset mamma would just walk calmly and quietly out of the house. She'd come over to me and put her arms around me. "I love you, Mel. I'm proud of you, son" was all she'd say.

But pretty soon I'd be hugging her back and sobbing, "Oh, I'm sorry, mamma! I want to be good, really I do." My heart was just melted whenever they gave me love and tenderness. And to this day it's the only thing in the world I can't resist.

So you and I agree that we're not supposed to judge someone who is sinning. We'll just let the Lord worry about how to make him repent from all the things he's doing wrong. But exactly what is our attitude supposed to be if we don't condemn him?

Well, I believe we're supposed to see him through the eyes of Jesus, to have the same attitude about him that the Lord does.

It really was hard for me to learn this. Even though the Lord was so super-merciful to me, it was hard for me to be merciful to someone else. (Sometimes I think that I'm a prime example of stupidity. It takes me so terribly long to learn something.)

There was a little lady in Timor, one of our team members, who just irritated me to death. She used to be so spiritual—until she went off the deep end, that is. I don't want to tell you what her name is because I don't want to embarrass her. So just for fun let's call her Mamma X.

Boy, the Lord really used her tremendously those first few years after the revival started. Through her ministry alone at least five people were raised from the dead.

One of them was a man in the island of Semau who had

been murdered—his enemies had poisoned the water he was drinking. But when the family called Mamma X to the house to pray for the dead guy, the Lord raised him back to life. She also prayed for a little baby girl in Soe who had been dead for twenty-four hours, and the Lord did the same wonderful miracle for her. Of course, there are several more stories, but I don't think I have time to tell you about all of them right now.

Tha main thing I want to tell you is what happened to Mamma X as a result of the Lord using her this way. Unfortunately she got terribly puffed up and proud about all of her spiritual gifts. When two American ladies visiting Timor found out about the mighty miracles the Lord had done through her, they were thrilled.

"We must take you back to the States with us," they told her. "Everyone will see how extraordinarily the Lord has used you, and they will be amazed."

I'm very sorry to say that this went to her head—their flattery really spoiled her. She went around bragging to all her friends that she was going to America. She actually thought she was better than all the rest of us. She got so proud that it was downright sickening! It made me very upset.

One day I just couldn't stand it any more. I ran into the little room where I was staying, flopped down on my bed, and buried my face in the pillow.

"Oh, Jesus!" I yelled in my heart, "why do You use that horrible lady! She just brings embarrassment to the fellowship here. Why in the world did You ever use her in the first place if You knew how she was going to end up? Jesus, You made a horrible, terrible mistake!"

Jesus let me pour out all my angry thoughts. And then very gently but firmly He spoke in my heart: "Honey, you don't have to feel so bad that I used her; you can be thankful. If I use someone as 'horrible' as she is, then I can use you too. But if I had a very high standard and would use only perfect people, then you'd never have a chance. You despise Mamma X because you don't understand My whole plan in her life.

"Let Me tell you a little story," He went on. "Once upon a time there was a farmer who had an apple orchard. One day He took his little son with him to have a look at the trees. 'How do you like them?' the father asked as they strolled around together hand in hand.

" 'Oh, father, they're just awful!' the little boy cried. 'These stupid trees don't give nice apples at all—just these tiny little green things. Oh, father, I think we'd better cut them down!'

"But the farmer just smiled wisely to himself as he lovingly stroked the back of his apple tree. He could see what his little son couldn't. In a few months those 'tiny little green things' would be big juicy apples. But for now, those apples were growing just the way they were supposed to, and the farmer was very pleased. They were just the perfect size for this stage in their development.

"And now, Mel, honey, My dear son, let Me tell you something plainly." The Lord's voice was more gentle than ever, so tender that it cut deep into my heart. "You're very upset at Mamma X because you don't like the 'little green things,' the attitude of pride in her life. You're upset because you don't see her through My eyes.

"She is actually at just the right stage in her growing process; I've known all along that she'd be going through this stage. But I also know she won't stay this way. She'll keep growing into something much better. I can see not only the present but also the future, and I can see what a beautiful work of art My love is going to make of her life.

"Mel, honey," Jesus was whispering now; I had to strain to hear Him. "Would you like to know My opinion of Mamma X? Look in your Bible at Song of Solomon 4:7."

Do you know what I found after I had opened to the right page? "You are altogether beautiful, my darling, and there is no blemish in you." I was shocked. I never knew she was *that* precious to Jesus.

Oh, I was terribly, terribly ashamed of myself. My attitude toward her was so different from the Lord's attitude. Now it's a little bit embarrassing to tell you this, but I felt so ashamed I actually got up off my bed and crawled *under* it! I guess I didn't even feel worthy enough to lie on the top.

I remember I cried as if my heart were broken. I finally realized that *I* was the one that needed to be changed, not Mamma X. I had to ask Jesus to forgive me for my lack of love and understanding and for not accepting her the way He did.

(Now actually, Jesus' prediction that Mamma X would be beautifully transformed was completely accurate. He did wash all that pride out of her life, and she has since grown into a very sweet and humble Christian. Today the Lord is once again using her life in a wonderful way for His glory.)

Seeing other people through Jesus' eyes, concentrating on the beautiful finished product that they are becoming with God's help—this is what Jesus means when He tells us to love other people the way He loves us (John 15:12).

This is a supernatural, divine love; we can't do it by ourselves. As with everything else in the Christian life, we have to depend on the Holy Spirit to fill us and empower us before we can bear this beautiful fruit of love.

The Lord Jesus has asked us to open our whole life to Him to love Him with all our heart, soul, mind, and strength. But every bit as important is His command to love our neighbor as we love ourselves (Mark 12:31). We can't do one if we're not willing to do the other; those commandments go hand in hand. We don't really love Jesus if we refuse to love each other in that divine way we've already talked about. And unless we love Jesus completely, with every speck of our being, we'll never have the power to really love each other either.

I found a real good source to back up what I'm trying to tell you: the Bible. Just listen to this: "If anyone says 'I love God,' but keeps on hating his brother, he is a liar; for if he doesn't love his brother who is right there in front of him, how can he love God whom he has never seen? And God himself has said that one must love not only God, but his brother too" (1 John 4:20, 21, Living Bible).

10

Greater Works than These

One day the Lord told Team 17 to go to the little island of Rote fifteen miles south of Timor to preach the gospel. So they obediently hopped into a little sailing boat that we call a *perahu* and asked the captain and his crew to push off from the shore. (Actually this boat is nothing more than a large canoe with a huge sail attached to the side. It seats fifteen people. It has no lower deck. Everyone just sits out in the open and either gets burned by the sun or whipped around by the wind.)

Well, unfortunately, on this particular day the wind decided that he was going to give those guys a good beating. They had only sailed a few miles out of the harbor of Kupang before they realized they were headed straight for trouble.

Every year just at that time, at the beginning of the rainy season in November, a certain spot in the sea between Timor and Rote becomes a whirlpool. Three currents coming from three different directions meet at that spot. And when the wind is blowing just the right direction, the water starts to churn so violently that it's impossible to pass that place alive. Every year people who attempt it are drowned.

When the poor sailors and the team members set out from the harbor, it looked like a nice day. Everything was calm. But without any warning at all, an awful wind came up. It was driving them straight toward the whirlpool. Trying as hard as they could, they couldn't steer away from it. Huge waves were slamming into the helpless little boat. Its rim was only a few inches above the surface. The men worked frantically trying to bail out the water with tin cans. But how could they compete with such a horrible storm?

The poor captain was yanking on the ropes attached to the big sail as hard as he could, trying to keep the boat balanced. It seemed like any minute the sail was going to topple over from the force of the wind. The boat would sink, and of course they'd all be drowned.

Suddenly in the middle of all the confusion the team leader tapped the captain on the shoulder. "Sir, I have a message from the Lord. If everyone will quit what they're doing and sit down, Jesus will calm the storm. But you've got to stop trying to save yourself first."

"Who are you?" the captain demanded angrily.

"I'm a servant of the Lord Jesus Christ."

"Have you ever been in a storm like this before?"

"No. In fact, I've never even been in a boat in my whole life."

"Then get out of my way, stupid! You make me sick, acting like you know everything!"

The team leader patiently kept quiet. But the angry waves pounded all the harder and the wind blew even more violently. It was getting worse—much worse. But by now the men were so tired that they couldn't hold out much longer. It was obvious that in a few minutes they would all be dead.

When the team leader saw that the captain and his crew were really desperate, that they'd given up all hope, he spoke again. "Okay, are you ready to let my God handle this situation? Will you quit trying to save yourself?"

The captain knew they were going to drown sooner or later. He might as well let this crazy fool have his way. Finally he nodded.

"Then everybody sit down! Quit bailing the water. Drop the sail rope and quit trying to balance. My God is not going to do this miracle until every one of you quits working. Otherwise you'd try to claim the credit for yourselves."

When the last sailor had dropped his tin can and was huddling in the bottom of the boat, the team leader spoke to the storm! "In the name of the Lord Jesus Christ, I command you waves to be calm and you wind to stop blowing!"

The instant those words were out of his mouth, the miracle happened. The captain and sailors watched spellbound as those violent waves stopped in midair and suddenly sank into the sea. One second they were six feet high, and the next second, *whoosh!* Down they went before their very eyes until the whole sea was flat. And those angry winds! Well, they simply disappeared—as if heaven had opened its jaws and suddenly swallowed them.

There was a deafening silence. The water looked as peaceful as a gentle little pond. There was no evidence that there had ever been a storm except for the white foam that lay scattered over the surface.

The captain and his sailors couldn't resist such an obvious proof of God's power. They were fanatic Moslems, but right there in that little boat, before it even reached shore, they gave their hearts to Jesus. The captain told the team that he was going to rename his boat *Hidup Baru,* which means "New Life." And from that time on he would always give any of his new Master's servants a free ride, taking them any place they wanted to go. That was his way of saying thank you to the God who had saved him.

I don't know when my papa got saved, but I do know that the whole time I was growing up he loved Jesus with all his heart. My papa has really influenced my life. Even when I was just a little boy (a naughty brat, like I told you before), I was amazed to see how faithful my father was to the Lord Jesus. He was never afraid to obey the One he loved.

Papa wasn't a great evangelist. I mean, he didn't go all over Timor telling people about Jesus. He was just a simple schoolteacher. But he decided that he was going to give the best witness he could in the insignificant place God had put him. So he told all his pupils about Jesus, and a lot of those little kids got saved.

He also witnessed to his neighbors. In the little villages of Timor that are too remote to have a pastor of their own, the schoolteacher is responsible for preaching the sermon on Sunday. My papa didn't hesitate to preach the real gospel—how all of us are sinners and we can only come to God by trusting Jesus' shed blood to save us. Well, as a result almost everyone in his village was converted.

It really made the pagan priest who lived nearby mad when he found out who was responsible for making him lose so much business. So he determined to destroy papa. He used his most powerful witchcraft against him, but somehow those curses could never work. Over and over again the Lord miraculously protected my father.

Finally when he saw his black magic was powerless, the witch doctor decided to try to destroy papa by turning all the people against him. So he spread a rumor through all the villages of that area that my father was responsible for the serious drought they were having. The gods were angry at him, so they wouldn't give any more rain until the people got rid of papa.

It was at the end of the dry season. Usually by that time the land is very thirsty, just aching for a good rain. But that year the drought had been unusually severe. There hadn't been a drop of rain for months. The ground was scorched and cracked. The leaves had dried off the trees and even the grass had shriveled up. Worst of all, the wells were almost completely dry. At the village spring where everyone went to collect their drinking and cooking water, the poor people would have to wait for hours for the spring to drip out just a few buckets of water.

Papa knew that the witch doctor's accusation was enough to make the people furious at him. They were desperate enough to do anything to get some rain. So he really prayed about the situation, and praise the Lord, God gave him wisdom to know exactly what he was supposed to do.

On the thirty-first of October Papa held a big outdoor meeting. He invited all the Christians of his village plus the witch doctor and his followers. And at that meeting in simple faith, he put his God on the spot. Like a modern Elijah he dared God to prove that His power can still work miracles today. He turned to the witch doctor and said, "I am going to dig a well right now. My God is going to give me water. If He doesn't, then I will renounce my Christian faith and become a pagan just like you." (Believe me, that took courage! I sure don't recommend that you do this unless you're positive the Lord has told you to.)

Papa and a few of his friends grabbed some old shovels and began to dig. They had hardly gotten started—their hole was only three feet deep, in fact—when suddenly water started to bubble up inside the hole. Pretty soon it filled the hole and overflowed, racing down the hill, gushing out across the cracked, barren land. That water just didn't stop flowing. Right there in front of everyone's eyes the Lord created a brand-new stream, and to this day it has never run dry.

I was on my brother-in-law's team, Team 36, for two years. During that time I saw the Lord do some amazing things. As we crisscrossed Timor holding revival meetings in scores of different little villages, we saw thousands of people repent and turn to Jesus. But we also saw the Lord do some tremendous miracles of healing.

One night in a little village near Fetuat after the revival service, we were sitting in the living room of the pastor's house praying for the sick. Only one person at a time came into the house for prayer; the rest of them stood around outside waiting for their turn. It was a lot easier to do it this way than to stand at the front of the church praying for a long line of sick people.

At the pastor's house we could drink tea and eat cookies while talking to the people, and we didn't have to stand up for hours at a time.

One of the people we prayed for that night was a typical little old Timorese lady in a handwoven *sarung,* something like a long wrap-around skirt. The lady might have woven it herself using red, orange, yellow, and black thread. She was wearing a longsleeved blouse that—I was going to say it buttoned down the front, or maybe snapped. But I can't say that because Timorese ladies don't use either buttons or snaps. They use safety pins. For some reason they think it's pretty to have a whole string of big silver safety pins running down the front of their blouse. (Even at the fanciest meetings they always show up with a bunch of safety pins.)

Her blouse had bright pink and purple flowers splotched around on it. Of course it clashed unbelievably with her red and orange striped *sarung.* But Timorese ladies don't care. The wilder the combination the better, as far as they are concerned.

It was obvious what this poor little lady's problem was. She had a huge goiter, about the size of a papaya hanging from her chin. (In case you don't know how big a papaya is, her goiter was the size of a cantelope.) But before praying that the Lord would heal her, the different members of our team ministered to her spiritually. We have a principle that before we'll pray for someone to be healed, he must first be willing to make everything in his life right with God. We have found out by experience that after a person has been healed spiritually and emotionally, it's no problem at all for him to receive a physical healing too.

But sometimes it takes hours for a person to get all his hang-ups cleared away. Fetuat, where we were ministering, was right in the heart of the area where the Alauts live, and everybody we talked with that night had a connection with demonic power in some way or another. We just patiently took our time though, spending as long with each person as he needed.

Well, finally when the little old lady had renounced all the demonic power that was binding her and had asked Jesus to take control of her life, we felt she was ready to be healed. My brother-in-law laid his hand on top of her huge goiter and asked Jesus to take it away.

While we were praying, the most amazing thing happened: that goiter sunk back into her throat as if it were melting away. My brother-in-law said he could actually feel his hand moving closer and closer to her neck. By the time we opened our eyes after the prayer was over, that lady's neck looked completely normal! There was no goiter to be seen anywhere!

The lady grabbed at her throat, and when she found out that the awful, ugly thing had disappeared, she was so happy she screamed. (She probably thought, like I did, that it would take Jesus a few days to fix her up completely.) I don't blame that dear lady for screaming. I probably would have done the same thing myself.

Not too long ago (in January of 1973) a man and his wife were walking home at the end of a long hard day of work. They had been weeding their rice fields outside their village in Java and they were terribly hot and tired and dirty. As they trudged up the road, they passed their neighbor's house. All at once they noticed that someone inside the house was crying very hard. They were shocked. The wailing was so loud that something terrible must have happened.

They knocked on the door, but there was no answer. The sobbing just continued louder than ever. Finally they pushed open the door and walked in. There in the dim half-light of the little room they could make out a form lying motionless on the bed and a woman kneeling on the dirt floor beside it.

"What on earth is the matter?" the couple asked.

"Oh, my poor husband has died," the lady sobbed.

"How long ago?"

"I don't know. Several hours at least. I've been crying ever since."

The couple walked over to the bed. The corpse had no breath and no pulse. In fact, it had already become so still that they couldn't move its arms or legs. It didn't take too many brains for the farmer and his wife to figure out that the lady was right. Her husband was dead.

"Oh, we're so sorry," they said, trying to comfort her. "We must go back home right now and wash up and change our clothes. Then we'll tell all our friends what has happened and make the arrangements to have him buried. But first we want to pray for you."

Now actually, the farmer and his wife were brand-new baby Christians. Four months before, they had been fanatic Moslems. But since their conversion they were trying to learn everything possible about the new faith.

"Our pastor told us last Sunday that Jesus never changes," they went on. "If He could bring dead people back to life two thousand years ago, He can certainly do it again for us today. So let's ask Him to let His perfect will be done."

They bowed their heads and reverently began to talk to the Lord. "O dear Lord Jesus, if You want to, please raise this man from the dead. You know how this sweet lady needs her husband. Otherwise just comfort her real good; wash all the grief from her heart. You know what is the very best, so we just commit this situation into Your hand."

Then they said good-by and walked outside the house. They had only gone about sixty feet when all of a sudden the lady ran to the doorway. "Come back! Come back!" she yelled.

"Why? What's wrong?"

"As soon as you left, my husband started to move!"

By the time they got back inside, the man was sitting up in the middle of the bed, smiling from ear to ear. "What happened to you?" they asked.

"Oh, I died and went to heaven to be with Jesus. It was so wonderful up there. When Jesus told me I had to go back to earth, I didn't want to because we were having so much fun together. But Jesus insisted. He told me not to feel bad though,

161

because pretty soon He would come to earth Himself to bring both my wife and me home to live with Him forever."

"Well, that's nice," the couple said. "But while you were up there having so much fun, your poor wife was crying her heart out down here. So why don't you be a nice husband and comfort her and love her up real good?"

Well, the farmer and his wife went on home and washed up and ate their supper. And that's the end of their story.

But that's not the end of the Holy Spirit's story. He channeled His mighty power through the Lord Jesus. And He channeled it through Team 17, papa, and the farmer and his wife. The glorious fact of the matter is that the Holy Spirit doesn't have favorites; He wants to pour His miraculous power through your life as well. He wants to use you too to demonstrate to the world that His power can still do the same wonderful works today that it did when Jesus lived on earth two thousand years ago.

Now that's exciting! You have to admit it's an awful lot of fun to watch the Lord use you to do big exciting miracles. It's one of the super bonuses of being filled with the Holy Spirit—ministering to other people with His beautiful gifts; gifts like faith and wisdom and healing and miracles (I Corinthians 12:8-10; see also Romans 12:6-8).

But I know some people who have gone off the deep end. All they can think and talk about are the gifts. It's their favorite aspect of being filled with the Spirit.

They aren't so hot on the other aspects—like the fruits of the Spirit or letting the Lord control them entirely. But actually, these parts of the Spirit-filled life are a terribly necessary foundation.

In the last few chapters I've been trying to explain four different parts of the Spirit-filled life. The chapter about letting this wind blow was supposed to show how we need to give every part of our life to Jesus. The next two chapters were about taking every part of His abundant life for ourselves. The one about the kingdom of love was actually talking about how to put the fruits of the Spirit into practice. Now we're finally ready to talk about the most exciting subject of all—the gifts of the Holy Spirit.

We stuck this subject at the end of the line for a reason. You see, the Lord can't really trust us with His power until we're in a right relationship both to Himself and to other people. We have to be fully under His control, experiencing His whole new way of life, and we have to be a channel of His love to other people before we'll be ready to be a channel of His mighty miracle-working power. Otherwise we won't be mature enough to handle that power. We'll just make a horrible mess, and the devil will end up getting the glory.

Now please don't get me wrong. I'm not saying that the gifts aren't important. They are. They're awfully important, in fact. It doesn't do much good to love somebody if you don't have the power to bring them to Jesus. The reverse is true, too. The Bible says that all the power in the world isn't worth a single penny until it is combined with love (I Corinthians 13:2). So love and power must always work side by side.

The gifts of the Spirit are actually the *works* of Jesus being reproduced in the lives of His followers. Lots of times while He was on earth Jesus said that it was His wonderful *works* that proved He was the Son of God (Luke 7:20-22; John 5:36; John 10:36-38; John 14:8). That same principle still holds true today. Very often in a pagan country, people will never repent and come to Jesus until they see those mighty works. We can preach all we want, but it takes the demonstration of God's power to convince them.

The eastern end of the island of Java is a good example of this. Thousands of fanatic Moslems live there. When I call them fanatic, I mean fanatic. They out-and-out *hate* Christians, and they don't try to hide it either. If they get the chance to kill somebody who believes in Jesus, they pat themselves on the back and think they've done God a tremendous favor. They are totally convinced that Islam is the only true religion in the world.

163

It's a known fact that Moslem countries are the hardest mission fields in the world today. I have a missionary friend who worked for thirty years in the country of Malaysia and saw only one person get converted that whole time.

I know of only one way to bring Moslems to Jesus: prove to them through miracles that the power of the Lord is stronger than the power of the devil. In my country most of the Moslems also worship Satan. They know how strong his power is. They are too smart to ever follow a God that is weaker than the devil. So if they are going to become Christians, they must be convinced that Jesus is more powerful. Otherwise, once they started to follow the Lord, the devil would get mad and beat them up. This is a serious matter of life and death.

In 1970 one of my friends accepted the challenge from the Lord to work with the people in East Java. He held open-air meetings, and beside preaching about Jesus he prayed for sick people. Hundreds were healed: blind people, cripples, demon-possessed people. When the Moslems saw the miracles with their own eyes, they immediately were convinced about Jesus. My friend told me that even *hadjis,* men who had made their holy pilgrimage to Mecca, would jump up onto the platform the very first meeting they attended, grab the microphone, and tell everybody that from that day they were going to follow Jesus, because they had seen what the Lord's power can do. (Whenever a Moslem does something, he does it all the way. When he knows something is real, he wants to jump in and take it right away.)

Praise the Lord, thousands of these fanatic Moslems have been converted. More than forty churches have been established. Believe me, that takes a miracle! The farmer and his wife I told you about before, who prayed for the dead man to be raised, are from this area. Their story is just a little example of the tremendous revival taking place there this very minute.

So you remember how my papa challenged God to give him water just like Elijah did? Well, as a result of the Lord doing that beautiful miracle, the witch doctor (or pagan priest) who had caused all the trouble got converted! God's power was too strong to resist. This is one of secrets of the Indonesian revival. We've not only preached about God's power, but we've also demonstrated it by letting Him do mighty signs and wonders through us (Romans 15:18,19; I Corinthians 2:4).

There's another secret I haven't shared with you yet. When our teams go into the little villages to preach the gospel, they train all the converts to become disciples. When the team finally leaves the village to go somewhere else to preach, another new team has been born. These new baby Christians band together and go off in a different direction to tell people about Jesus. They too win people to the Lord and in turn start new teams. But the Lord also uses them to do the very same miracles of healing or casting out demons that their mother team has done.

You see, my people have learned an important lesson. In God's eyes, one person is not more spiritual than another. If God uses one person to do miracles, then He wants to use everyone else as well. The people in Timor don't think of the team member as special. They don't try to follow after or idolize certain *people*. Instead they follow after Jesus. It has never occurred to them that miracles *wouldn't* happen in their ministry if they too are right with God.

"Truly, truly, I say to you, he who believes in Me, the works that I do shall he do also; and greater works than these shall he do; because I go to the Father" (John 14:12).

This Bible verse blows my mind. Do you realize what Jesus is saying here? Every one of us, if we really believe in Him the way we are supposed to, will do the same fantastic things He did when he lived on earth. We will experience God's power flowing through us in that same way that it flowed through Jesus. Miracles will result from our life that are beyond our wildest dreams.

Jesus wants to use *me* to do His works.

And my friend, He wants to use *you*.

The Lord's plan is for you to cleanse lepers the way He did. He wants you to pray for sick people to be healed, and then to step back and watch Him restore them to perfect health. He wants you to be so confident of His power and authority that you will be able to cast out demons, and even to raise dead people back to life again (Matthew 10:8).

Has anyone ever told you to read John 3:16 trading the words *world* and *whosoever* for your own name, to make the verse more personal? The verse then reads something like this (cross out my name, and stick in yours instead): "For God so loved *Mel Tari*, that He gave His only begotten Son, that (if) *Mel Tari* believes in Him (he) should not perish, but have eternal life."

All Christians like John 3:16. They believe Jesus really meant business when He said it. They believe He was talking about *them*. But Jesus was just as sincere when He said John 14:12. In fact, maybe He was trying to sound even more emphatic. He knew we'd have trouble believing what He was saying, so He even stuck a few *truly, truly's* on the front.

Now try reading this verse, replacing *he that* with your own name. "Truly, truly, I say to you, (if) *Mel Tari* believes in me, the works that I do shall he do also; and greater works than these shall he do, because I go to the Father."

That's pretty powerful. Why don't so many of us see Jesus' works being reproduced in our own life? Well, I believe it's because we don't have simple faith. Before the Lord can use us, we must concentrate on getting to know Him. We must know Him so well that we'll know exactly what He wants to use us to do in each situation. We must be close enough to Him to hear His voice if He says, "Go to the hospital this afternoon and pray for your Aunt Mary. I am going to heal her broken back; the doctors will be amazed." Or, "This thunderstorm is not glorifying Me. The devil is trying to use it to keep My people away from church. Command it in My name to leave, and command the sky to become blue and sunny. I want to do a miracle with the weather right now." Or, if your husband brings fifteen people home for dinner without warning you, Jesus might say, "I know you don't have enough hamburger casserole to feed all the extra people. Commit the food to Me; ask Me to do a miracle right now, and I will create food where there was none before."

I believe that as we are wholly committed to the Lord and love Him with all our heart, as we let His gentle breeze blow unhindered in our life, moving us closer and closer to our Loved One, the Lord will make sure that sooner or later His mighty miracles will be performed through us. We will do the works of Jesus.

But we can only do as much as the Lord has given us personally to be responsible for. All of us must join together as a team, as the different members of the magnificent Body of Christ. In love we must work side by side through the power of the Holy Spirit. With our combined efforts the works of Jesus will be performed many thousands of times over.

Yes, the gentle breezes that have worked in the lives of thousands of Christians all over the world will unite to form a mighty, rushing wind. And with one final spurt of power, that great wind will sweep around the globe, kindling the fires of revival everywhere, preparing the earth for that great day when the King of Kings will descend from heaven to establish His everlasting Kingdom. Praise the Lord!

11
Getting Ready
for the Bridegroom

My, those angels are busy! Look at that tall one over there shoving those tables across the floor. He's trying to arrange them in long lines, I guess, in this huge, glowing room. There are a few over to the left carrying big stacks of golden plates. And do you see that guy just coming through the door now? He's wheeling in a tray of golden goblets that he's probably going to place around the table. And, oh, look! That angel with the sweet face standing over there by the window with a huge armful of roses. It looks like he's going to put one beside each place.

I get the idea they're getting ready for a big party, don't you? The aroma drifting out the kitchen door right now sure makes me hungry! Those heavenly cooks are really outdoing themselves this time. From the smell of it, all their skill is going into those kettles.

But the banquet hall isn't the only place they're working. There are angels all over the place—in the great entry hall, in the corridors, in the big storehouse, in the throne room. Oh, look here, see all those angels polishing up the great throne? They're putting two velvet cushions on it instead of just one. And they're laying out the most magnificent royal robes, the ones studded with jewels. Candles are being lit all over this already dazzling room. It looks like a great coronation ceremony is about ready to begin.

Over in the bridal chamber the most elaborate preparations of all are being made. Angels are spraying every corner of the room with the sweet fragrance of love. Some are looping garlands of flowers from the chandelier to the wall lamps to the archway of the door. Others are spreading crimson petals across the floor to make a brilliant carpet. A great coffer of dazzling jewels is being placed in the center of the floor. That is probably the dowry the Bridegroom is going to give this Bride—beside the supreme gift of Himself, of course.

All of heaven is astir with excitement. Any minute now the Lord Jesus will rush from its holy halls to claim His Bride. Then, robed in magnificent glory, the two of them will enter the heavenly gates to begin a life of unequaled joy together.

But first, the Bride must get herself ready, dressing in a gleaming spotless garment of white linen. "Hurry, hurry!" the angels call. "Your wedding hour has almost come!"

Heavenly messengers are being sent out across the earth, alerting God's children that their Bridegroom will be coming to take them home to Himself any minute.

God wants all His children to get this important message. So in 1973 He sent one of His messengers to the terribly primitive, Stone-Age island of West Irian (maybe you call it New Guinea).

One day a Christian lady was out digging oubi roots in her garden. (That's the Stone-Age equivalent of a grocery store. If somebody wants to eat, they simply dig their groceries out of the ground.) This lady was keeping up with the current styles. All she was wearing was a grass skirt around her waist.

Her two little boys were playing happily beside her. They were all having a wonderful time, when suddenly the lady looked up. And who should she see standing in front of her but a very strange-looking man. He was wearing a long flowing white robe that reached the ground. The lady was astonished. She had never seen anyone dressed that way in all her life.

But when he started to talk, his message was even more strange! "I am a messenger from heaven, sent by the Most High God. He told me to tell you to go back to your village. Tell everyone to get ready, because the King is coming!"

Without any warning he disappeared right in front of her eyes. Well, the lady had enough sense to realize that something stupendous had happened. She'd better not disobey this divine command. So she threw her great big digging stick to the ground, grabbed her two little boys by their hands, and raced back to the village shouting to everyone, "Get ready! Get ready! The King is coming!"

"Who is the King? What should we do to get ready?" everybody asked.

"I don't know. The man didn't tell me. But maybe the missionary would know."

He did know. Praise the Lord that the C&MA (Christian and Missionary Alliance) missionary was there just when the people needed him to tell them about Jesus and the Second Coming.

A few years before, a small group of people in the island of Alor were in desperate need. So again the mighty Ruler of heaven dispatched His angels with a proclamation of joy. But let me tell what had happened first.

The Lord had started a revival in that island. It all began with a certain man (he was a schoolteacher) whom the Lord sovereignly touched. Without any human influence at all Jesus revealed Himself to this guy and explained to him the way of salvation. When he gave his heart to the Lord, he was filled with the Holy Spirit's power. He got a real desire to lead other people to the Lord. So he walked up and down those terribly steep mountains talking to everyone about his Jesus. Pretty soon a small band of new converts had joined him.

Well, the so-called Christians in that area got really mad. It made their blood boil to see how different this new group

170

acted. They didn't practice witchcraft anymore. They didn't drink or even smoke anymore. Instead, they seemed just delighted with their new life in Jesus.

The so-called Christians hated the real Christians. They couldn't stand their guts. So they actually beat those new converts with sticks and then dragged them off to the police. Those wicked guys told lies about the "Jesus people," saying they were insane and should be locked up in jail. (Actually the so-called Christians were scared because the real Christians' ministry was so contagious. They were afraid that pretty soon there would be a big epidemic of people forsaking their sin and going all-out for God.)

It was a time of real persecution for that new group of believers. They desperately needed the Lord to comfort them and give them strength to go on. So one afternoon they all gathered outside in the front yard of their church to pray.

Suddenly the sky was crowded with angels. Overhead, just above the tops of the tall coconut trees, scores of them flew back and forth. They were singing. Their magnificent anthem rolled out across the village.

All hail the power of Jesus' name!
Let angels prostrate fall,
Bring forth the royal diadem
And crown him Lord of all!

(This was not a vision. Anyone walking by the church could see the angels. And people all over the village, including the Christians' enemies, heard the singing.)

Greater and greater the volume of their song grew. "Crown Him! Crown Him! Crown Him Lord of all!"

Soon the little group felt as if they'd been transported; they were caught up into the chambers of heaven itself. It seemed that they were no longer seated on the hard ground. Instead they were kneeling around the throne, lost in the splendor of His glory, crying out from the depths of their hearts their worship and adoration for the One who loved them.

So soon, so soon the time would come. They'd leave this poor, miserable world forever, and all their suffering and persecutions would be transformed into glistening jewels to cast down at their Savior's feet. Yes, those trials that had once seemed so hard to bear would become invaluable—precious tokens of their love for their mighty Lord and King.

It was during the first week of the revival that the Lord gave us an impelling order. That night, at one of the spontaneous meetings that were constantly being held in the big church, a girl named Jakoba was sitting in the service along with hundreds of others. (She was the girl who spoke in English just a few nights before when the revival started. Do you remember her from *Like a Mighty Wind?* See pages 26,27.) All at once, while everyone else was singing, the Lord spoke in her heart. "Get up, Jakoba. Leave your seat and walk outside the building."

She obeyed. Then He added, "Now look up in the sky."

As Jakoba looked, there in the night sky, surrounded by a host of brilliant stars, she saw a beautiful angel. He was huge, about twenty feet tall, it seemed, and in his hands he held a golden trumpet. As Jakoba watched, the big angel raised the trumpet to his lips and stood there poised.

It was then that Jakoba heard the Lord's voice speaking so distinctly, echoing like thunder through the sky: "Tell My people to get ready and to prepare! Tell them I am coming back very soon!"

This has been the pulsebeat of our hearts as we've gone all over our country telling people everywhere about the Lord. I believe that this is the deepest purpose of the Indonesian revival. The Lord is doing such a mighty work among us because He wants to prepare His people, His precious Bride, for His very soon return.

"Get ready!" Jesus urges us. But how? What can we do to get ready?

This is actually what we've been talking about the whole way along in this book. The only thing we can do to get ready for our Bridegroom is to be normal, healthy Christians; to live our Christian lives the way He planned. And what is Jesus' plan for us?

To let Him fill us with His Holy Spirit so that we can experience His abundant life.

To live just as close to Him as possible so that we can be living demonstrations of His love and power to others.

To love Him passionately, with every part of our being, and to treasure Him above all else.

Yes, that's what a bride really is: someone who cherishes her bridegroom so deeply that she is willing even to suffer for him. No hardship is too great as long as she can be one with her beloved. You know, in the days ahead we may very well be required to prove if we love Jesus that much. These end days are very exciting, it is true. But they're also difficult. Satan is on the warpath. He's super-mad because he knows his time is short, so he's out to plague and persecute Jesus' loved ones. The Bible actually promises that if we love Jesus with all our heart, we will be persecuted (Philippians 1:29; Acts 14:22; 2 Timothy 3:12).

In these last days many people are getting visions and prophecies about calamities that are going to come on the world. In Timor we have had visions like this since the beginning of the revival. But these messages didn't emphasize the problems we are going to go through. God always told us, "Don't worry. I'm going to take care of you. No matter what happens, I will see you through!"

I believe that even in the middle of awful trouble God wants to make us overwhelmingly triumphant. He wants our faith in Him to be so strong that even then we can enjoy His abundant life. That's the great strength of Christianity— even when we're suffering, we can be bubbling over with the joy and contentment that comes from living with Jesus.

But why do we have to suffer right before Jesus comes back?

Well, I don't really know. Maybe it's to make us all the more anxious to see Him, and maybe it's to make us appreciate the purity and beauty of our new home. It will be such a relief to leave the hardships of this sinful old world.

But anyway, we can be sure of one thing: with total confidence we can trust Jesus to carry us safely through any difficulty. He will never fail us. His love will be there to protect us and to meet every need we could ever possibly have.

Hallelujah! Our little trials are just a prelude to a life so fantastically wonderful that it staggers our imagination. When I first got saved, I used to try to figure out what heaven was like. I'd dream up the most fabulous life-style I possibly could. "Is this what heaven will be like, Jesus?" I'd ask.

"No, honey, it will be much better than that."

So then I'd really screw up my brain. I'd think up all kinds of tremendous additions to my first version. "Okay, then is this what it's going to be like?"

"No, honey, it's going to be even better," He'd say.

Then I'd let my imagination run away with me. I'd dream and dream until I got dizzy. "O Jesus!" I'd say, all out of breath. "Surely, heaven can't be any more wonderful than this!"

"Honey," Jesus would answer me, "you might as well give up. Heaven is far, far better than that. It's so wonderful you'll never be able to comprehend it with your puny little brain. Eye has not seen, nor ear heard, neither has it entered into the heart of man the things I have prepared for those who love Me" (I Corinthians 2:9).

Wow! God sure must have something stupendous up His sleeve! An incredible future is about ready to burst upon us. If heaven were all we had to look forward to, that would be enough to make us go out of our minds with excitement.

But my friend, you and I have an even greater destiny than that. You and I have been chosen to be the beloved ones of the Lord Jesus Christ Himself. We will have the tremendous honor of seeing Him face-to-face and knowing Him intimately. He has chosen us to reign with him throughout all the ages of eternity (Revelation 3:21). We will actually sit with Jesus in His throne, honored as His most beloved Queen and clothed in the garments of His royalty.

O the sheer delight of being one with Jesus! Day after day we will gaze up into His face, drinking in His sweetness and His overwhelming beauty. The radiance of His smile will warm us to the depths of our beings as He whispers to us those deep, profound secrets that we could never quite understand here on earth.

Hand in hand He will lead us down the corridors of glory; with greatest pride He will show us off to the angels, obviously overjoyed to possess such a beautiful Bride. And because we are the darling of His heart, there isn't anything He will withhold from us. Those magnificent treasures He inherited from His Father He will share with us as well— His power, His honor, His splendid glory.

Yes, any minute now the climax of history will begin. The Lord Jesus will rush from the halls of His palace in heaven to claim us as His Bride. Then robed in magnificent glory, the two of us will enter the heavenly gates to begin a life of unequaled joy together.